The Political Economy of Forest Use and Management

The Political Economy of Forest Use and Management

M.V. Nadkarni
with
Syed Ajmal Pasha and L.S. Prabhakar

Sage Publications
New Delhi/Newbury Park/London

First published in 1989 by

Sage Publications
M–32 Greater Kailash Market I
New Delhi 110 048

Sage Publications Inc
2111 West Hillcrest Drive
Newbury Park, California 91320

Sage Publications Ltd
28 Banner Street
London EC1Y 8QE

This study was financially supported by the Indian Council of Social Science Research, New Delhi. However, the Council is not responsible for the views expressed here.

Published by Tejeshwar Singh for Sage Publications India Pvt Ltd, phototypeset by Mudra Typesetters, Pondicherry and printed at Chaman Offset Printers, Delhi.

ISBN: 0-8039-9591-1 (US-hbk.) 81-7036-134-6 (India-hbk.)
0-8039-9592-x (US-pbk.) 81-7036-135-4 (India-pbk.)

Contents

List of Tables

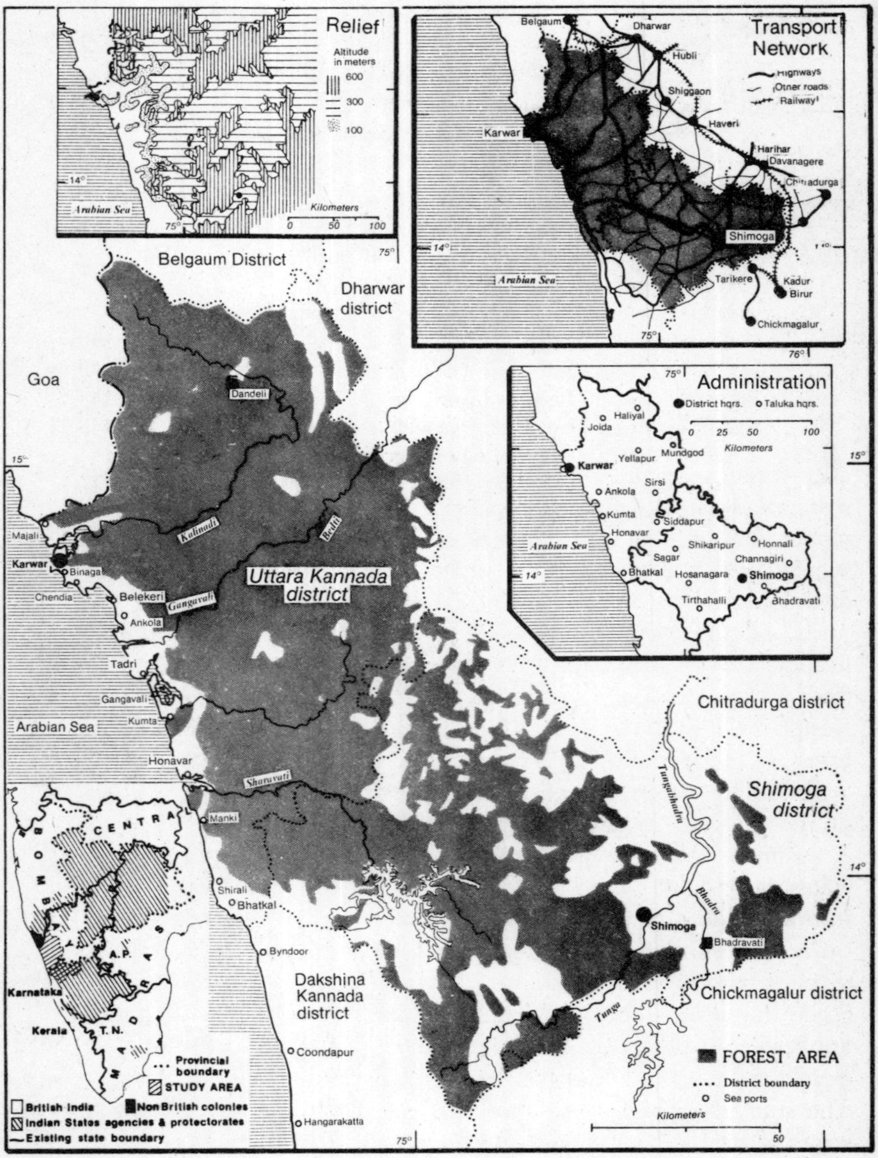
Relief
Altitude in meters
600
300
100
Arabian Sea
Kilometers
0
50
100
Transport Network
Highways
Other roads
Railway
Belgaum
Dharwar
Hubli
Shiggaon
Haveri
Karwar
Harihar
Davanagere
Shimoga
Tarikere
Kadur
Birur
Chickmagalur
Arabian Sea
Administration
District hqrs.
Taluka hqrs.
0 25 50 100
Kilometers
Haliyal
Joida
Karwar
Yellapur
Mundgod
Sirsi
Ankola
Kumta
Siddapur
Honavar
Shikaripur
Honnali
Sagar
Channagiri
Bhatkal
Hosanagara
Shimoga
Tirthahalli
Bhadravati
Arabian Sea
Belgaum District
Dharwar district
Goa
Dandeli
Kalinadi
Bedti
Majali
Karwar
Binaga
Chendia
Belekeri
Gangavali
Ankola
Uttara Kannada district
Tadri
Gangavali
Kumta
Arabian Sea
Honavar
Sharavati
Manki
Shirali
Bhatkal
Byndoor
Dakshina Kannada district
Coondapur
Hangarakatta
Chitradurga district
Tungabhadra
Shimoga district
Bhadra
Shimoga
Bhadravati
Chickmagalur district
Tunga
FOREST AREA
District boundary
Sea ports
Kilometers
50
CENTRAL
BOMBAY
MADRAS
A.P.
Karnataka
Kerala
T.N.
Provincial boundary
STUDY AREA
British India
Non British colonies
Indian States agencies & protectorates
Existing state boundary

Foreword

In recent years the relationship between ecology, environment and sustainable use of natural resources in the course of economic development has become a live topic of discussion in the literature on the subject. It was in the context of this interest that a small unit was established in the Institute for Social and Economic Change for the study of Ecology Economics, and Professor M.V. Nadkarni was placed in charge of the same. This book is among the noteworthy products of this new research unit in the Institute. The study, though focused on Karnataka, is of wider interest written as it is in the larger context of forest use in the country as a whole and national economic development.

The interesting feature of the study is its contribution to an analysis of the political economy of forest use and management. Political economy is brought into the picture because, as Professor Nadkarni states, 'a problem in the economics of resource use transforms itself into a problem in the political economy of resource use when the ordering of ends in terms of their importance is done not by a given decision maker, but through a struggle between vested interest groups'. Since the struggle between different vested interest groups is also applicable to other instances of resource utilisation and economic development, the methodology of this study can be of general interest. The study presents an analytical account of the struggle at various stages of forest resources utilisation beginning from the pre-commercial to the dominance of industrial use, and also probes into possibilities of reaching an enlightened stage of resource use which reconciles the conflicting interests consistently with the needs of conservation.

This book is interesting for its combination of historical analysis with a field study of the contemporary situation in forest resources utilisation. The political economy of forest use cannot only be restricted to the struggle between three interested parties which are normally dealt with in discussions on the subject, i.e., local interests, larger economic interests covering the country as a whole, and the State as an overall determinant in the subject. Professor Nadkarni's special contribution lies in the class analysis of the highly inequitable use of forests by the different interest groups within the local economy and the local population. This is in contrast with the normal treatment given in studies of forest utilisation wherein local population and local interests are considered as a homogeneous whole, while the State itself is identified with the industrial and commercial interests of the larger economy. Professor Nadkarni's study is also notable for its emphasis on local interests leading to the deterioration of forest resources and the multiplication of denuded and degraded forest areas and wastelands. In the light of the study, it appears that it is not the forest department as such which is primarily to blame, but the failure of both local economic interests and larger commercial and industrial interests to give due emphasis to the need for taking sufficient account of the sustainability of resource utilisation by both these local and nationally extensive economic interests. All local economies in the forest regions such as the one dealt with in this study are not tribal economies, and we cannot mechanically extend our sympathy for tribal people to cover all forest regions and hold the forest department responsible for the mal-utilisation of forest resources.

Professor Nadkarni's approach leads him to expose the weakness of both the extreme positions—the populist and romanticist position on the one hand which makes for our going back to the pre-commercial past and handing over forests to the locals, and, on the other hand bureaucratic and technocratic solutions which rest wholly on the presumed omnipotence of the forest department. The study emphasises the need for a more eclectic and objective approach to the problem. It stresses the importance of evolving new institutions tailored to meet the requirements of different situations which will ensure local people's participation as well as the use of the expertise and support from the forest department so that both the local people and the department can work together rather than at cross purposes.

While the study draws pointed attention to the crisis situation of forest utilisation for economic development, it ends on an optimistic note because of the recent breakthrough even in local public opinion towards a recognition of the need for sustainability of resource utilisation not concentrating purely on short term considerations. Another reason for this optimism is the recognition by the Central Government of the need for conservation along with utilisation of forest resources, and the setting up of a special Ministry at the Centre which ensures taking into account environmental considerations in sanctioning new projects of economic development. The new price policy for forest products which takes into account the cost of regeneration and sustainability of resource supply in the future has also succeeded in putting a damper on the short period factors in the tapping of forest produce by powerful vested industrial and commercial interests operating on a national scale. The vast area of deforested land and other waste lands available for afforestation as also the possibilities of significantly increasing the productivity of Government managed forests, point to the potentials which can be realised. How far institutional innovations would evolve to transform this potential into realisation, depends on the innate genius of our people and the forest department.

I have no doubt, therefore, that this scholarly work will prove interesting and useful, and hopefully capture the attention of a wider audience covering social workers, forestry experts and social scientists.

Bangalore **V.K.R.V. Rao**
March 1988

Preface

The deterioration of our forests both in quantity and quality has been receiving wide attention among academics and people at large. There is a general consensus now that forests are not a matter of interest to forestry experts and the forest department alone. This has emboldened me—hardly a forestry expert—to make this encroachment. Incidentally, this is an encroachment into economic history too, since my formal training and qualifications hardly justify it. I have obviously taken advantage of the permissive atmosphere regarding encroachments very much like the local people living in a forest region.

If the outcome of my encroachments has turned out to be productive, I owe it to the inspiration from Professor V.K.R.V. Rao who personally does not believe in academic barriers, and induced me to take an interest in broader environmental issues at a time when I had confined myself only to agricultural economics. I am further indebted to him for kindly agreeing to write a Foreword to this book and enhancing its value.

Forests have different uses and functions to different sets of interest groups. The rationale of this study is based on the contention that the problem of reconciling diverse ends with scarce means is not resolved in neoclassical economic terms, but through a political struggle between interest groups. It, therefore, constitutes a problem in political economy.

This problem is studied at two levels, complementary to each other. First, it is at the historical and regional level focusing on the struggle between three interested parties—the locals, the commercial interests of the larger economy and the Government, covering the period from around 1800 to 1980s. A theoretical framework of the stages of development is used to analyse different stages of forest use and management, and the impact of the struggle both on the health of forests and the local economy. Though a forest region in the Western Ghats comprising of two districts—Uttara Kannada (North Kanara) and Shimoga—are taken up as a case study, the discussion takes note of changes in Karnataka state and in India as a whole.

At the second level, the study of political economy focuses on the class character of the contemporary local economy itself and its forest dependence, through a survey of households in selected villages. Contrary to common belief, the locals were not alienated from forest use in spite of the high level of State regulation, thanks to their prolonged struggles with the forest department. But they have been alienated from forest management and regeneration. The local economy still depends significantly on forest use outside the market framework, but most of the benefits accrue to the two richest classes of the rural society to support the cultivation of commercialised garden crops. Yet the locals have not taken any interest in the regeneration of forests under their access and use, at least till recently. The class differentiation within the rural society emerges as an important factor affecting the quality of forest use. It is possible that in some other areas locals have made better use of the forests taking into consideration regeneration and conservation. Nevertheless, this study has shown that any general and unqualified prescription on populist lines ('Give forests back to local people, and everything will be all right!') could lead to disaster.

The concluding part of the study takes a synoptic view of both aspects of the political economy problem and draws out policy implications. Alternative institutional forms have to be evolved involving the locals in the management including the poor peasants and the landless, if the forest question has to be resolved to the satisfaction of all interested parties.

The study was undertaken with the support of a financial grant from the Indian Council of Social Science Research.

During the planning stage, I benefited from the comments of Professor V.M. Rao, Harsh Sethi, and two anonymous referees of the

Council on the draft project proposal. Discussions with Dr Suryanath U. Kamath and Professor Madhav Gadgil respectively on the historical and environmental aspects of the study region were also a great help at this stage.

Dr Kamath kindly gave access to several useful documents including the old issues of Kānadā Vritta. G.V. Joshi helped in obtaining other documents of historical interest on Uttara Kannada from Revenue Offices and from the old files of elderly political leaders in the district.

Stimulating discussions with Dr G.V.K. Rao were very useful, particularly on the problem of afforestation in wastelands.

The officials of the Forest Department of Karnataka were very helpful both in Bangalore and at the field level. They gave access to available information asked for including the Annual Administration Reports and other statistical material. Discussions with S. Shyam Sunder and some of his colleagues—M.N. Jayakumar, P.D. Gaonkar, G.S. Prabhu, R.M. Palanna, Siddappa and others—were useful in seeking clarifications on a variety of questions. Shyam Sunder was also kind enough to lend a few books of historical interest. At the field level, I should particularly mention Pravin Chandra Pande, the dynamic Deputy Conservator of Forests of the Sirsi division from whom we learnt many things. His colleagues—A.M. Annaiah, K. Uday Kumar and others—were extremely helpful.

Above all, the people of villages which we visited have contributed a lot to this study. They were frank, cooperative and hospitable. We learnt a good deal from them, including K.M. Hegde, a progressive farmer from Bhairumbe village and a leader in constructive and organisational activities in the region.

I have been ably and sincerely assisted by Syed Ajmal Pasha and L.S. Prabhakar. They accompanied me during my field trips, took the responsibility for conducting structured interviews and stayed much longer in the field. They also listed and tabulated field data. The notes prepared by them particularly on field impressions were helpful in Part II of the volume.

The invitation by Olle Edqvist and SAREC gave me an opportunity of presenting a preliminary draft of Part I at three seminars in Sweden. Discussions with Edqvist and M.R. Bhagavan, as also comments made in the seminars at SAREC, Department of Economic History of the University of Umea and at the Research Policy Institute, Lund, have been quite helpful.

The entire study was first released for comments in September

1987. In revising it for publication, I have benefited from critical comments and suggestions made by the participants at a seminar at our Institute where it was presented, and also by Madhav Gadgil, William Stewart, Ramachandra Guha, B.G. Varghese and an anonymous referee of the publisher. I am grateful to all of them and also to Professor C.H. Hanumantha Rao and Dr Yoginder K. Alagh for their kind words.

B.G. Kulkarni has prepared the map presented here. It gives an idea of the location of the study region—Uttara Kannada and Shimoga districts, along with the extent of forest area, important towns and other details. The location of the region is shown in relation to the erstwhile Bombay Presidency, the old princely State of Mysore and also the present State of Karnataka.

I have a special word of appreciation for T S Vanishree, our efficient stenotypist, for her neat and prompt work.

While I heartily thank them all, none of the above is responsible for the views expressed and the analytical approach used here or for any errors therein.

August 1988 M.V. NADKARNI
Institute for Social and Economic Change
Bangalore

Part I

The Local *vis-à-vis* the Larger Economy and the State

Chapter One

Introduction

Why Political Economy?

Forests have several uses or functions which often compete with each other. Forests are scarce and are becoming increasingly scarce in the face of pressure on them. The situation apparently fits neatly within the framework of the economic problem as defined by Robbins[1] except that it is more complex. Robbins was concerned with a given decision maker, who would decide towards which end he would use the scarce means at his disposal. This was a comparatively simple situation amenable to a solution in terms of the neat optimality criteria of neoclassical economics. Imagine a situation where the scarce means have alternative uses to different sets of users, who compete—or more accurately—struggle for the dominance of the scarce means. The problem is no longer purely economic and is hardly amenable to neat solutions of neoclassical economics.[2] The reconciliation—if it can be so called—between ends and scarce means is decided in the arena of political economy. The solution to an economic problem is feasible because the 'ends are capable of being distinguished in order of importance,'[3] facilitating a choice. But *a problem in the economics of*

[1] The economic problem in terms of his definition is one of reconciling ends and scarce means which have alternative uses. *Cf.* Lionel Robbins, *An essay on the nature and significance of economic science*. London: Macmillan, 2nd ed., 1935, p. 16.

[2] This is because, as Arrow showed long ago, individual preference orderings cannot be aggregated in such a way as to have a reasonable social ordering; he showed how difficult, if not impossible, it was 'to extend the concept of individual rationality prevalent in economic theory to collective or social rationality'. *Cf.* K.J. Arrow, *Social choice and individual values*. New York: Wiley, 1951, as quoted in G.R. Feiwel, The potentials and limits of economic analysis: The contributions of Kenneth J. Arrow', in G.R. Feiwel (Ed.), *Arrow and the ascent of modern economic theory*. London: Macmillan, 1987, p. 22.

[3] Robbins, *op. cit.*, p. 14.

resource use transforms itself into a problem in the political economy of resource use when the ordering of ends in terms of their importance is done not by a given decision maker, but through a struggle between vested interest groups. This struggle need not be equitable. As a result, the benefits of a resource use may be cornered by one class, while the environmental costs may be borne by another. In such a case, total benefits cannot even be compared with total costs to judge the worthwhileness of a resource use. In other words, normal economic analysis breaks down.

As is well known, forests help in maintaining a balanced environment and more specifically help in maintaining soil health and productivity of natural watersheds. They support many known and unknown organisms and wildlife. They provide the means of sustenance, food, fuel, fodder, and raw material for human use, which may be more or less commercialised depending on the phase of the development of the concerned region. The crucial question is according to whose relative valuation of these different uses or functions, the actual use of forests would be decided.

Among the interested parties, there are the locals, that is, those who live in the forest region and depend on the forests for their sustenance. Apart from fuel wood, fodder, raw material like bamboo for artisans, and minor produce like honey, local use of forests can take the form of clearance of forests either for shifting or settled cultivation. Even if not cleared for cultivation, forests support local agriculture by providing green manure and fodder, preventing soil erosion and maintaining ground-water recharge. The locals, however, are not a homogeneous group and the class differentiation in the local economy influences not only the distribution of benefits from forest use, but the quality of forest use itself, as we shall see in the course of this study. The locals include tribals and other local poor having little or no land, farmers and landed gentry having rich garden lands. There are also merchants and forest produce processors who serve the larger economy. Even if locally settled and belonging to the local community, they are part of the larger economy being its agents or employees, and have to be distinguished from the locals.

Commercial and industrial interests of the larger economy also find the forest resources immensely useful. Hardwood or timber is needed for construction, furniture, the railways and the like, while softwood is required for paper and pulp mills and for packaging. They try to dominate the use of forests both through influencing the government and through setting up their own agents in the forest regions. These interests arise from and determine the process of commercialisation of the forests, which is but a part of the transformation of both the regional and the national economy from a pre-capitalist to a market oriented mode of production. This process also involves integration of the forest region with the larger—national—economy and fundamental technical changes in how forest resources are treated and exploited.

The state or its concrete form—the government—is the third interested party in forest use. Presumably, it is interested in the welfare of all citizens and tries to promote the greatest good of the largest number. Since promoting economic growth makes available a large amount of resources to it with which it can govern, and since such growth is also basic (if not a sufficient condition) to improving the levels of living of its people, the modern state is always concerned about maximising the rate of economic growth. But modern economic growth takes place through commercialisation and capitalist development, involving exploitation of natural resources and integration of regional economies into the national economy. The state facilitates this process. Presumably, the state is interested in the long-term as well, and would like to provide a corrective to the myopic view of private commercial interests. While permitting the exploitation of natural resources, the modern state tries to regulate its use to prevent its squander. Though the state's basic preoccupation is with the interests of the larger or the national economy as a whole, it also faces the challenging task of reconciling short-term commercial and growth interests with long-term interests of conservation, and of regulating as well as accommodating the local use of forest resources in the face of pressures from the larger economy. The regulation of local use need not be exclusively for accommodating commercial and industrial interests. It is also to provide a corrective where the local use is found to be wasteful and against the long-term interests of conservation. Thus when neither commercial nor local interests ensure conservation of wildlife and areas considered ecologically sensitive, the state steps in to ensure this. As such, the state finds it absolutely indispensable to have a control over the use of forest resources, unless its responsibility is to some extent relieved by local initiative and institutions oriented to conservation and sustainable use.

If a complete control over forest resources could place the government in the same ideal position as that of a rational decision-maker of Robbin's perception, who could order all alternative uses in order of importance from the point of the economy as a whole without involving any conflict of interests between different parties, there would have been no place for a study of political economy of forest use and management. The government becomes one of the three main actors in the struggle for the use of forest resources, responding to pressures of other actors and also to technical changes in the larger economy. The character of the state as well as its ideology regarding forest use and management undergo a change from time to time. The larger political changes like takeover by a colonial power interact with technical changes. These changes not only alter the conditions affecting the demand for and supply of forest resources, they also alter the relative status of different interest groups.

A historical study of forest use and management in this context is not, therefore, restricted to neoclassical perceptions of economic history.[4] It also has to focus on the conflicts generated by technical change and by the attempts of the government to integrate the forest region into the larger economy. Our objective here is to study this process in a forest region, the conflicts it generated and its impact. In other words, a major aspect of the study of political economy of forest use and management is a study of how and in what stages a forest region was opened out and exploited by the larger economy, what effect it had on the region itself and its agriculture both in the colonial and post-independence period, and how the government tried to resolve the conflicts. This is discussed in the first part of this book, the focus of which is on the struggle and reconciliation between the local and the larger economy. The period of study covers broadly the nineteenth and the twentieth centuries, since the process of technical change and commercialisation started in the last century itself in India. The process is studied here with reference to two contiguous districts which form part of the Western Ghats (mountainous regions) in Karnataka, namely, Uttara Kannada (North Kanara) and Shimoga. However, the discussion is by no means restricted to this region, and takes care of changes in Karnataka as well as India.

Since the local economy itself is class differentiated, its use of forest also has to be studied from this angle. The second part of this book adopts a micro level view of the contemporary local economy to

[4] As expressed by Robbins: 'The economic historian is not interested in the changes of ends and the changes of means in themselves. He is interested only in so far as they affect the series of relationships between means and ends which it is his function to study.' *Ibid.*, p. 40.

understand how different rural classes benefit from forest use. The concluding part of the book takes an integrated view of both the levels of the study, and draws out the policy implications.

Conceptualising the Process

The process being studied here has three dimensions: technical change, commercialisation and integration of the local (forest) region into the larger economy. All these three aspects go together. The process can be conceptualised as involving four historical stages. In chronological order, they are: pre-commercial-cum-pre-capitalist stage, initial commercial stage, highly commercialised (or industrial stage), and the advanced or enlightened stage of systematic and rational management with due regard to conservation and regeneration. As we shall see these stages are overlapping and not mutually exclusive, but can be identified mainly in terms of their dominant characteristics. The purpose of this conceptualisation is analytical, and to see how far the actual observations agree with or differ from theoretically expected stages. It may also be added here that this conceptualisation views the historical process from a modern perspective. But when we apply this to actual empirical periods, deviations can be observed and analysed.

The pre-commercial-cum-pre-capitalist stage of forest use can be said to be one when the market for forest produce had not yet developed from the larger economy and the use was mainly local in a non-market framework. As such, forest resources—produce, if not the land itself—were considered unlimited and a free gift of nature, the only cost being one of going to forests to gather forest produce; even this cost was hardly monetised. There were some exceptional items of forest produce which were considered scarce and had a good market (e.g., ivory and sandalwood). But the commercial use of major forest produce was only marginal during this stage, if at all. It was believed that the resources were so abundant that the question of regeneration did not arise. The local use, apart from meeting the needs of local population in respect of fuel, food, fodder, green manure and timber for construction and implements, was such that it could be considered extravagant by modern standards. This involved burning the entire forest areas to convert wood into ash for fertilising land and in the process also clearing it for cultivation on a shifting basis. The primary reason for this extravagance was that on the whole forest resources were not perceived as scarce.

However, in quite a few instances, particularly where the local economy had developed a settled character and both agriculture and livestock economy came to depend significantly on resources under common use, local conventions and institutions were also developed to prevent unsustainable use of such resources and to ensure an equitable access to them.[5] This was easy where the local social structure itself was fairly harmonious and egalitarian, but not when it was dominated by one class or community to the detriment of others.[6] We must remember that pre-commercial-cum-pre-capitalist societies were not necessarily any more homogeneous and egalitarian than the subsequent societies.

The significance of this stage of forest use is that the local use of forest land and forest produce has continued within a non-commercial framework through subsequent stages, though the local conventions and institutions to ensure sustainable use have not necessarily continued even where they existed. The local demands on forest land for grazing and for cultivation, and on forest produce for fuel wood, green manure and timber for construction and implements, continue to be a source of pressure in a non-market and political framework, without a corresponding enthusiasm for reviving the old conventions and institutions.

The process of commercialisation of forests started when they began to be used by the larger economy particularly in respect of major

[5] For an example of how through tradition and religious veneration forests were protected by local communities, see Madhav Gadgil and V.D. Vartak, 'Sacred groves of Western Ghats of India', *Economic Botany*, vol. 30, 1976, pp. 152–60; Ramachandra Guha, 'Scientific forestry and social change in Uttarakhand (U.P.)', *Economic and Political Weekly* (henceforth *EPW*), Vol. 20 (45–47), Special Number, November 1985, esp. p. 1940; M. Gadgil and Prema Iyer, 'On the diversification of the common property resource use by the Indian society', paper presented at the seminar on Common Lands Issue, 23–24 November 1987, at Dharwad, organised by Samaj Parivartana Samudaya, Dharwad, and the Centre for Ecological Studies, Indian Institute of Science, Bangalore (unpublished).

[6] Gadgil and Iyer (*ibid.*) mention certain conditions favourable to sustainable use of CPRs: '(a) the number of parties sharing access to the resource is small, (b) the parties sharing access repeatedly interact with each other over a long period, (c) such parties are linked to each other by bonds of kinship or reciprocation in contexts additional to the resource use'. Obviously, such conditions did not prevail everywhere.

produce. This ended the perception of abundance and brought in the feeling of scarcity. Outside interests began to assert their control over forests and impose restrictions on local use. Political subjugation of the region to the larger economy was a necessary condition for this, which was easily achieved. This adversely affected the role of local communities in managing local resources, particularly forests, to the extent that they did play such a role. Thus the history of commercialisation of forests is also a history of conflicts between local and outside interests and the alienation of locals from the management of local resources.

During the initial stage of commercialisation, the forest produce was subjected only to marginal processing like cutting and shaping of timber and used by the larger economy for construction, railway sleepers, etc. During this stage the larger economy mainly demanded hardwood and not softwood for industrial processing. Even when this demand for timber became prominent, the need for a systematic management of forests began to be felt both to regulate local use and to ensure regeneration of commercially more valuable forest produce. Though production forestry could have the potential to end scarcity and reduce conflicts through an increased supply of forest produce, this was not realised. When the natural forests were cleared for commercial plantations, the source of supply of fodder, fuel and green manure was cut off for the locals.

Meanwhile, the more advanced stage of commercialisation of forests was seen when industrial capitalism directly dominated forest use. The forest produce began to be processed as a raw material for industry. The main demand shifted from hardwood to softwood for the paper and pulp industry. Even the demand for traditional produce involved a significant technical change. For example, sandalwood was now demanded mainly as a raw material for extracting oil and the demand for teak was from the plywood industry rather than from direct consumers. Large and highly mechanised saw-mills replaced small mills using primitive machines, and were often combined with plywood making. The difference between the initial and highly commercialised stages is that in the former, commercialisation was chiefly under the auspices of merchant capital, and industrial capitalism was yet to develop; while in the latter stage, the process of commercialisation of forests was largely promoted and controlled by industrial capitalism. However, the role of merchant capital particularly in timber trade and processing continued in the latter stage, though subjugated to capitalism.

Often the timber merchants themselves set up industrial processing units.

The advance of commercialisation was thus a process of both technical change and change in the organisation and control of forest economy. 'Technical change' here corresponds to the Marxian concept of 'forces of production'. However, 'production' here is not confined to aspects of regeneration of forest produce or production forestry alone, but covers extraction as well. Technical changes or forces of production relevant to commercialisation of forests extend well beyond forests and refer to forces in the larger economy itself. Similarly, relations of production in the forest use should cover relations between the forest region and the larger economy as expressed through the control of forests, and not merely those existing within the sphere of production. Expropriation is involved here, but not of formal ownership as such of forests (which may or may not have been with the locals before commercialisation), but of local access to forests for direct use. Management itself has, therefore, a double character here—one of regulating or preventing free local access (with a bearing on relations of production or organisation), and one of promoting regeneration and productivity of forests for commercial use (with a bearing on technical change or forces of production).

The process of commercialisation of forests was initially triggered by technical changes outside the forest region, that is, in the larger economy. The organisation was then adapted to meet the increased demand for forest produce. This organisation had to initiate technical changes within forests such that regeneration of forest produce and supply on a sustained basis were ensured. Thus, exogenous technical changes led to internal changes as well. However, even before this process could establish itself, further exogenous changes took place almost with a sudden burst, and the process of adaptation and adjustment broke down. This threatened to give a jolt to the whole process and create a crisis in both the regional and the larger economy—a crisis in which the whole environment was threatened and neither the local nor the industrial needs were met and technical change slowed down.

Moreover, what further complicated the process was that with all the technical and organisational changes, the non-commercial local use of forests could not be completely eliminated. The local communities continued to exist, and so did their economy which was dependent on forest use. The larger system could neither destroy the local economy nor absorb it. The management of conflicts with the local economy depended on the nature of the organisation adopted. The organisational set-up adopted in the wake of commercialisation in India was increased state control over forests. The state stood for promoting technical change and considered its control and its own direct responsibility for production forestry as the most effective form of organisation in India. There could be alternatives to it, for example, involving the peasants themselves in production forestry. The nature of the organisation has implications both for the intensity of conflicts generated and for the production base of forestry, as can be seen from the historical account that follows.

We can also conceptualise—at least as a social goal to be pursued if not as a historical stage already achieved—an enlightened stage of forest use and management when the conflicting interests are reconciled to the greatest good of all not just in the short run, but more essentially in the long run. At this stage it would not only be realised that forest resources need to be managed basically from the wider perspective of environmental protection and that there has to be a limit to exploitation of forests by industries, but actual forest use and management would take place in that way. And yet it would not amount to a reversion to the pre-commercial stage. The productivity of forest use would be so increased and land use so planned that both the needs of industry and local people would be met on the basis of a proper appreciation of the scarcity of forest resources used and a provision for their adequate regeneration so that a sustainable use is ensured. Forest use and management would be integrated with strategies of economic development and resource use in general, based on a due recognition of the role of environment in long-term development. Obviously this would be possible only through the active co-operation and participation of the local people, since even at this stage a complete elimination of the local economy and its absorption by the larger economy cannot be visualised.

This is a stage yet to be realised, and even a definite and strong tendency towards it cannot be taken for granted as something inevitable or preordained. Innovations would be required not only in technology to save forest raw material, but also in economic incentives/disincentives and in institution building to reach this stage. Since a crisis situation has already emerged, the need for long-term survival for all concerned could lead to corrective steps before it is too late. Particularly when the local people begin to realise their stake in achieving the enlightened stage, a trend towards it can be hoped for. Fortunately, there are already signs of this in India. Thus the enlightened stage need not be regarded as one that will take centuries to realise, but something that can be attained within a foreseeable future.

Chapter Two

Pre-Commercial Stage

Our Study Region

Before discussing the actual operation of these stages of forest use and management, it is advisable to know more about the study region. Of the two districts being studied here, Uttara Kannada is a coastal district with the Arabian Sea to its west, and Shimoga is in the interior. The Western Ghats rise steeply from a narrow coastal strip, and the main forest area in Uttara Kannada is in the mountainous or ghat section. The geographical areas of the two districts are 10,276 and 10,548 square kilometres respectively, with populations of 1.07 and 1.66 million respectively in 1981. The area under forests according to official figures—which does not necessarily reflect the area covered by trees—was 81 per cent in Uttara Kannada and 31 per cent in Shimoga in 1980–81. Today both have industries using forest produce—especially saw-mills and a paper and pulp mill each—though Shimoga has a longer history of modern industry. Shimoga has a railway line cutting across the whole district and a better network of communication than Uttara Kannada. Only a part of Uttara Kannada is served by a rail-head, there being no extension to it since 1918 when it was started for transporting timber.

The political setting of the two districts has varied markedly. Both came under the rule of the illustrious Hyder Ali and Tippu Sultan in the eighteenth century. When Tippu Sultan died in 1799 in a battle againt the British, Uttara Kannada came under direct British rule, whereas Shimoga was placed under the dynasty of Hindu Maharajas which had ruled Mysore earlier. However, the new princely State of Mysore came under indirect British rule. Though the British mode of forest management was in principle made applicable to the State of Mysore, in practice the rigour of this management seems to have been more lightly felt there than in Uttara Kannada. There is a long history of struggles against the Forest Department in Uttara Kannada which has been recorded in the local Kannada news weeklies.[1] A study of these struggles provides insights into the character of forest management, the nature of grievances and the actors involved. However, there is no such history of struggles in Shimoga against the Forest Department. The bitterness generated by grievances on forest issues, lent inspiration to the freedom struggle in Uttara Kannada[2] as it did in Thana of the same Bombay Presidency,[3] in which the former was included before the re-organisation of states in India in 1956. Unlike Thana, these districts did not have a tribal population to a significant extent. There were of course small communities (Vaddars, Siddis, etc.) who depended on forests as woodmen, tree cutters and timber carriers, in addition to depending on shifting cultivation (especially *Cumri*[4] Marathas). They did not however own or cultivate agricultural land. That is, the region consisted mainly of settled agriculturists, in spite of shifting cultivation being practised here and there. Yet the dependence on forests was vital to their agriculture and livestock. Thus, it was largely the owners of agricultural and garden land whose interests conflicted with British interests in forest exploitation. Though both Uttara Kannada and Shimoga illustrate the process of commercialisation and the conflicts it generated, our focus here will be mainly on the former both because it is more dominantly a forest region with a larger portion of its area under forests and also because of the greater availability of historical information about this district. To a great extent, conflicts in Shimoga were resolved and did not erupt in the form of open struggles because of the availability of a higher proportion of its area for cultivation.

We will now trace the course of regional development and the various stages of the process discussed earlier, with reference to our study region. It may be noted that though the stages can be demarcated conceptually, yet there are transitional periods where two or even more stages can co-exist. As such, it would be difficult to clearly

[1] Particularly, '*Kānadā Vritta*' (hereafter *KV*) of Kumta, old issues of which were available to the author.

[2] See Suryanath Kamath, 'Karanirakaraneya Hinnele' (Background to the no-tax campaign), *KV*, Special Memorial Volume, Kumta, 1982, pp. 181–86.

[3] See Richard Tucker, 'Forest management and imperial politics: Thana District, Bombay 1823–1887', *The Indian Economic and Social History Review*, Vol. XVI (13), July–September 1979.

[4] *Cumri* or *Kumri* is the local word for shifting cultivation on hill slopes or forest areas.

identify the year or even the decade when one stage ended and another began. We can only give broad indications.

The Pre-Commercial-cum-Pre-Capitalist Stage

In India, the legal ownership of agricultural land was a very complex issue, though superior rights in land marked by liability to pay land revenue were more easily recognised. But as far as forest land was concerned, it was more or less taken for granted that formal ownership was with the king or the feudatory chief of the region. Francis Buchanan, who travelled in this part of the country, wrote his diary in 1801 (that is, within two years after the control of the region passed into the hands of the British) and has mentioned the case of a 'Mahrattah Brahman' who came to 'Carculla' (Karkala) in Dakshina Kannada (South Kanara) some 250 years earlier and applied to the then ruling chief Byrasu Wodear for some hills to develop betelnut plantation in the valleys.[5/6] Once forest land was converted into garden, proprietary rights could be given. During the regime of Hyder Ali and Tippu Sultan, forest land was the property of the king. Naturally, its control passed into the hands of their successors along with the kingdom. It may be noted that, as a principle, private property in forest land was not unacceptable. Where, however, there was no record of private property, it was treated as government property, and such forest land accounted for the bulk of forest area.[7]

[5] Francis Buchanan, *A Journey from Madras through the countries of Mysore, Canara and Malabar*. Madras: Higginbothams and Co., 1870, Vol. II, p. 262.

[6] It is possible that such formal permission was not always necessary. Guha has quoted from an official handbook of the Forest Department issued in 1893 to say that during the pre-British days, 'anyone was accustomed, without let or hindrance, ... to clear jungle growth for cultivation wherever he listed'. *Cf.* Ramachandra Guha, 'Forestry in British and post-British India: An historical analysis', *EPW*, Vol. 28 (44), 29 October 1983, p. 1883; fn 6 on p. 1893.

[7] A formal notification was issued by the Collector of Kanara in 1811 to prove proprietorship in all lands covering forests too. Little forest land was claimed. The record for Supa forests at least showed that no claim on forest lands was put forward and the right of property in all the forests was taken as vested in the government. See D.A. Thomson, Deputy Conservator of Forests, *Working plan of Supa fuel resources*. Bombay, 1906.

However, there was a distinction between exclusive private rights over forest land and community rights over its produce. There was no alienation of the locals from the forest in spite of the state ownership of forest land during the pre-capitalist stage. This is evident from the travel account of Buchanan as well as from the representations made by the locals to the British government where they gave an account of the privileges enjoyed earlier,[8] and some of the reports prepared by the British officers in the early part of this century.[9] The locals had free access to forest land for grazing their cattle, fuel wood, wood required for agricultural implements and house construction, stakes required for hedges or fencing, and leaves (chopped branches) for green manure. Certain tracts around the village settlements were freely burnt and cleared, which were used for grazing cattle and also to maintain a buffer between forests and human settlement, so that the locals and their cattle were safe from wild animals and forest fires.

Even shifting cultivation was not considered illegal and improper. Buchanan has mentioned that hills cultivated in this manner (known locally as *cumri* cultivation) were regarded as private property, but the owners engaged hill dwellers (*Malaycudies*) for cultivation who were assigned cultivating rights in return for free labour on masters' lands. Their services were used mainly to cultivate *shamay* (Panicum miliare) or *ragi* (Cynosurus corocanus). Often the land was cultivated again in the following year, but the yields tended to be lower than in the previous year. They came back to cultivate the same land again after twelve years.[10] Though Buchanan has mentioned that no tax was assessed on such lands, gradually some of these lands came under revenue assessment. Prior to 1822–23, tax on cumri cultivation was included in village taxes, but from this year onwards it became part of land revenue.[11] For the sake of convenience, the tax was collected from regular holders of cultivated land, which must have given them more scope to exploit direct cumri cutters.

Even during the pre-capitalist stage commercial exploitation of forest produce was not totally absent. Though the locals had free access to forest land as mentioned earlier, valuable goods like sandal-

[8] See, for example, *KV*, 19 February 1920.

[9] See L.S. Swift, 'Revision Settlement Report of the Karwar Taluka', *KV*, 5 March 1917.

[10] Buchanan, *op.cit.*, p. 252.

[11] See *Gazetteer of Bombay Presidency, Kanara (Kanara Gazetteer)*, Part II, Bombay, 1883, pp. 188–89.

wood and ivory were under state ownership and control. There was also some trading in pepper, cinnamon, etc., collected from forest produce. Pepper was extracted both from forests and through cultivation in gardens. However, since the productivity of forest grown pepper could not be sustained without private proprietary rights, it sharply declined in importance.

Teak also gained in prominence during Hyder Ali's regime. He had set up a dock for building ships at the coastal town of Honavar in Uttara Kannada,[12] for which teak was needed. Teak was also used for fishing craft and small ships (*muchchvas*) built by local craftsmen long after (and also much before) Hyder's reign. However, restrictions pertaining to sandalwood and ivory were extended to teak as well, more because of its strategic rather than its commercial importance. Though teak was, to some extent, allowed for local construction, the state enjoyed a monopoly of export and import trade[13] both in valuable commodities like ivory and in commodities of strategic importance like teak. Apart from preventing the enemy access to such commodities, this was also to prevent spying under the guise of trading. Besides, both Hyder Ali and Tippu Sultan were well aware that trade and political control went hand in hand, with the East India Company extending its control all over India. In any case, the pressure on teak resources of the region during their regime could not have been anything comparable to what was to come with the emergence of Birtish commercial interests.

Apart from the fact that the demand from the larger economy on the forest resources was marginal, what were the local attitudes to forests during this phase? It is logical to expect that unless resources were regarded as scarce a conservationist attitude would not have prevailed, even if scarcity is not interpreted as being a product of the market alone. A favourable attitude to sustainable use can prevail when it is realised that local resources cannot last long when everybody uses them wantonly. Apart from general veneration and protection of individual species like Banyan and Peepul, Gadgil and Iyer

[12] Buchanan has recorded that the ships were meant for war; possibly they were for trade as well. *Op. cit.*, p. 297.

[13] This was in the sense that those who collected valuable forest produce had to sell only to state agencies, who alone had the right to sell it to officially approved traders who carried on import and export business. The *Kanara Gazetteer* mentions that 'teak, sandalwood and blackwood even when growing in occupied land have always been considered the property of the State', *Kanara Gazetteer*, Part I, 1883, p. 22.

have contended that there did exist institutionalised patterns of sustainable use by the locals before the British entry, as seen from the example of a cluster of villages near the coastal town of Kumta in Uttara Kannada itself. The village forests were communally managed by councils which either limited the quantity of wood extracted by each household in a season (in Kallabbe village) or permitted people to remove only dead and fallen wood (in Halakar village). These practices have continued there to date, according to them. Interestingly, these investigators have frankly reported that both these villages overexploited forests in other localities nearby, while protecting their own[14] (very much like some developed countries today who protect their own forests while importing cheap forest produce from other countries). Moreover, the coastal region of the district had much less forest and much more population pressure even in those days, including some perception of the limited nature of forest produce, which did not, however, prevail in the forest region proper.

An examination of Buchanan's travel diary leads to two unmistakable impressions about this stage as on the eve of British entry into the region. The popular impression that forests were treated as a community resource in the old days, equitably shared by all, did not appear to be true at least in a non-tribal region like Uttara Kannada. Whether theoretically ultimate legal ownership of agricultural land vested with the king/chief or not, *de facto* private property had come to be established in such land, and the benefit of forest produce like green manure and small wood accrued largely to the land controlling class. This class tried to dominate the use of forests near their own holding, establishing proprietary rights wherever they could on the hills nearby, which were used for *cumri* cultivation or pepper growing, and for collecting fodder and green manure. The agrarian structure was highly stratified, having two classes—those who controlled or owned land, and those who leased in and/or served as labourers. There was differentiation within these classes as well, due to the hierarchical tenure structure. The rice fields were almost always under lease, but betelnut and pepper gardens were under personal cultivation which was done with the help of both own and hired labour. This agrarian structure continued till about 1970.

The second impression relates to the condition of forests. Though forests at that time must have been much better stocked compared to

[14] Madhav Gadgil and Prema Iyer, *op. cit.* (see fn 5 in Ch. 1).

the present conditions, yet there were stretches of areas without trees or adequate grass cover even in this region. It is, however, difficult to say whether this was due to overgrazing or due to natural conditions, such areas being largely rocky laterite hills. But under natural conditions without overgrazing, even hills with shallow soil cover can yield at least *karada* grass used as fodder. Though, by and large, there was no pressure on the ecological balance during this stage, it was not so because forest use practices then were ecologically sound; it was more because the demand pressure from the larger economy was marginal. Stebbing has recorded that clearance of large tracts of forests for cultivation 'was having an adverse effect on the maintenance of the water supplies over considerable areas in some parts.'[15] As early as 1848, Cleghorn, who was Assistant Surgeon at Shimoga, had commented on the wholesale destruction of forests in the region due to shifting cultivation.[16] Signs of ecological deterioration were beginning to be seen.

On the whole, our theoretical conceptualisation of the precommercial stage is consistent with the empirically observed stage on the eve of British entry. In other words, it was not necessarily the idyllic stage which many romanticists recommend as worth returning to. Had there been a strong tradition of environmental care and perception of the scarcity of forest produce, it would have been reflected in the issues raised by social protests voiced in the subsequent stage of commercialisation. There was no evidence of such environmental consciousness in the local protests till the late seventies. Even if the pre-commercial stage contained seeds or forms of sustainable use in several communities, it has to be distinguished from the advanced stage of environmentally sound management, just as primitive

[15] E.P. Stebbing, *The forests of India*. London: John Lane, Bodley Head Ltd., 1921, Vol. I, p. 38. He has also observed:

> Long before our arrival the Indian ryot had begun in many parts to realise that water was diminishing, that streams and springs were drying up, and that areas which his ancestors had been able to cultivate were now becoming useless, for cultural purposes, owing to the—to him inexplicable—drying up of the streams upon which they had depended for irrigating the crops. Whole villages had to move to more suitable sites . . . .

Ibid., p. 36.

[16] Dietrich Brandis, *Indian forestry*. Woking: Oriental University Institute, 1897, p. 16.

communism has to be distinguished from the advanced stage of communism. The pre-commercial stage had no chance of adjusting to the industrial revolution and the demands of the larger economy. Obviously, a reversal to the pre-commercial stage is not feasible, even if considered desirable, though the principle of community involvement in afforestation and management of forests continues to be as relevant today as it was during this stage.

Chapter Three

Commercialisation—Initial Stage, Nineteenth Century

Commercial Pressure and Establishment of the Forest Department

Commercialisation of forests received a major thrust with the entry of the British into the region. British interest was mainly in teak which was needed by the Royal Navy as English Oak was almost entirely depleted before 1800.[1] Besides, teak was considered more durable. This placed a severe pressure on teak which was relatively abundant in Uttara Kannada. Though wooden ships declined by 1850, railway construction which was on a major scale since the 1840s kept up the pressure.[2] Railways, which covered the South as well during this period, not only created a demand for sleepers and planks for coach building, they also facilitated transport of forest produce to the larger economy. Though railway came to Uttara Kannada only in 1928 (and that too in a corner of the district through a link from Alnavar to Dandeli), and to Shimoga in 1899 which was extended further to Talguppa during the 1930s and the 1940s in phases, demand from the railways for teak and for other forest produce of these districts was generated much before. Earlier the major outlet for timber in Uttara Kannada had been through its ports, but with the improvement in road network more parts of the forest area were opened up to the interior of the larger economy.

The exploitation of forests under the Company rule was, however, hardly supervised in the country as a whole. The early years of railway

[1] *Cf.* R.G. Albion, *Forests and sea power*. Cambridge, Mass.: Harvard University Press, 1926, Chs. 3 and 9, as cited in Tucker, *op. cit.* (see fn 3 in Ch. 2), p. 277.

[2] Tucker, *ibid.*, p. 277.

expansion witnessed reckless and destructive use with absolutely no consideration for long-term interests.[3] A far greater number of trees was felled than actually required, including trees whose logs could not be utilised. This devastation was wrought by private contractors, both Indian and British.[4] This state of destructive use was admitted later by the British themselves. According to Stebbing, 'the first decades of the British occupation of India . . . . witnessed no check, but rather an enhanced rate in the destruction of fine timber forests'.[5] When this realisation dawned on the government, it was felt that at least valuable species like teak were not unlimited, making it conscious of the need to limit their exploitation within sustainable limits and to work scientifically for their regeneration and development. There was also an increasing official awareness of the wider environmental benefits of forests. According to a Statement of Forest Policy made by the Secretary of State in 1863, 'the proper growth and preservation of the forests is as important to government as the cultivation of any other crop which the soil produces and in some instances more important, since the destruction of forests would affect most injuriously the climate and perhaps the fertility of the soil.'[6] It was in this context that a decision was taken to form a separate Forest Department, and not merely regulate local use.[7]

Since 'the British of the period were unacquainted with the principles of forestry science',[8] the Department was set up with German expertise, with Dietrich Brandis as the first Inspector-General of Forests. Though the Forest Department was set up at the centre in 1864, the process had begun even earlier in the Bombay Presidency. The first attempt had been made in a very oppressive way and with a different motive altogether. Even as early as 1800, the Court of

[3] This was a part of the British tradition at least before the 1860s. There was, it appears, 'the near complete deforestation of England by the time the British established their empire. It is well known that the same British had totally deforested the Eastern United States and South Africa over the 18th and 19th century'. See Madhav Gadgil, S.N. Prasad and Rauf Ali, *Forest management in India: A critical review*. Indian Institute of Science, Bangalore, 1982, Mimeo, p. 21.

[4] Guha (1983), *op. cit.* (see fn 6 in Ch. 2), p. 1884.

[5] Stebbing, *op. cit.* (see fn 14 in Ch. 2), Vol. I, p. 38.

[6] As quoted by Tucker, *op.cit.*, p. 282.

[7] Guha has quoted the reminiscences of a British officer of 1902: 'The Forest Department was started because government became aware that the magnificent forests of India and Burma were being worked by private enterprise in a reckless, and wasteful manner and were likely to become exhausted if supervision were not exercised'. Guha, 1983, *op. cit.*, p. 1884.

[8] Stebbing, *op. cit.*, Vol. I, p. 38.

Directors of the East India Company had authorised the Bombay government to assume the right of felling timber on behalf of the Company. In 1806 an officer was appointed Conservator of Forests and was placed under Bombay, though the region (Kanara and Malabar) was at that time under Madras. In 1807 a proclamation was issued 'asserting the company's right of sovereignty over the forests, and forbidding the felling of timber by private individuals'.[9] Though the object presumably was to ensure

> *'a regular supply of timber for public purposes from the public forests, the Conservator of Forests . . . . assumed much larger powers and apparently he was supported by the Government . . . . No attempt was made to settle the boundaries of these forests . . . . The Conservator of Forests extended his operations over the whole country; he cut down and appropriated to the use of the Government, not only the trees of the private forests, but even those growing on cultivated lands. The proprietor was compelled to pay duty on the timber growing upon his own property when he made use of it for his own purposes . . . . For the regeneration and improvement of the forests the Conservator did nothing. It was complained of by all the local authorities . . . . In 1822, Sir Thomas Munro, then Governor of Madras, insisted on its being abolished, (observing) that 'no paltry profits in timber can compensate for the loss of their (people's) goodwill'.*[10]

After the abolition of the post in this way, it was created again in 1847 in the Bombay Presidency.[11] By 1859, there was one Assistant Conservator of Forests in North Kanara (Uttara Kannada), with a skeleton staff of only one clerk, two overseers and one *gumasta* (accounts clerk). By 1865, the district was divided into two forest divisions, one above and the other below the ghats, each under a Deputy Conservator with an increased staff.[12] These posts were first under the Revenue Department and later under the Forest Department after it was formed. But for a brief period between 1869 and 1885 when the Forest Department was dismantled as an economy measure,[13] it continued to grow in strength. Several princely States also organised their own Forest Departments under the broad policy

[9] Brandis, *op. cit.* (see fn 15 in Ch. 2), p. 9.

[10] *Ibid.*, pp. 9–10.

[11] Tucker, *op. cit.*, p. 281. Tucker has observed that it was the first such position in the country, apparently not aware of the 1806 episode.

[12] *Kanara Gazetteer, op. cit.*, (see fn 11 in Ch. 2) Part I, p. 22.

[13] *Cf.* C. Hayavadana Rao (Ed.), *Mysore Gazetteer*, Vol. III, Bangalore, 1929, p. 180.

framework of British forest management, though outside the jurisdiction of the Forest Act of British India.

Regulation of Local Use

Even before a systematic regulation of commercial exploitation of forests was attempted, official policy had begun curtailing the almost free use of forests and forest land by locals. The primary motivation was to prevent the squander of what was regarded as valuable by the larger economy. Such an official regulation of local use was in operation much before the Forest Department was formed, and was intensified thereafter. Though the tradition of State monopoly over sandalwood, teak and other valuable timber continued and more species of trees were reserved for government use, there was always a danger that wasteful practices of *cumri* cultivation which involved forest burning could harm the stock and growth of timber yielding trees. Thus, one of the first privileges to be restricted, during the rule of the East India Company itself, was *cumri* cultivation. In 1848, when Uttara Kannada was under Madras Presidency, *cumri* was prohibited in areas from where timber could be exported or where reserved varieties of timber grew. In the case of those who claimed it as a right because *cumri* assessment was entered in the records of their landholdings, the assessment was remitted and they were not allowed to exercise this right. In 1860, the government entirely forbade it for regular landholders, and allowed restricted practice in specified and permitted areas to only those hillmen who had no other means of livelihood.[14] After the transfer of the district to Bombay Presidency in 1862, the rule was slightly relaxed and clearings were allowed to some extent. But after this temporary lull, restrictions were tightened once again, and *cumri* area was reported to have declined from 7,785 acres (31.5 sq. kms) in 1863–64 to 844 acres (3.4 sq. kms) in 1878–79.[15] This proportion of land seems to be insignificant compared to the total forest area of about 2,271 thousand acres in the district then. It needs to be noted, however, that at a point of time, land actually under *cumri*

[14] *Cf. Kanara Gazetteer*, Part II, 1883, p. 189.
[15] *Ibid.*, p. 14.

cultivation may not have been large, but the total land affected year after year must have been more due to the shifting nature of cultivation. Moreover, the official statements referred to land assessed for revenue, which was a small part of the total *cumri* land.

Restrictions were also imposed in 1867 on the amount of *soppina betta* (referred hereafter as *betta*) land that owners of spice and betelnut gardens could possess. *Betta* lands refer to tracts of forest land held without proprietary rights by garden owners near their gardens which they could lop for leaf manure, fodder and fuel. Gardens were developed only in the valleys and the surrounding hill slopes were used for this purpose. In 1867, however, *betta* land was restricted to eight times the area of the garden. Moreover, cutting of trees without permission was penalised in such areas. While green leaves, small timber, firewood, etc., were allowed for own use, they could not be used for sale or barter.[16] Restrictions were also imposed on others who used forest produce. Carrying only headloads of firewood was permitted. Timber for house construction was supplied to locals at one-eighth to one-fourth of the market price, but they were not allowed to cut it themselves for free use.[17]

Gradually, restrictions were imposed even on trees within arable land or agricultural holdings. Teak, blackwood, sandalwood and other such trees in private holdings were declared as government property. In 1878, it was made specific that this principle applied to all future growth of such trees. Though other trees were considered the property of landholders, if they sold them they forfeited their claim to get any wood from government land or depots on a free or concessional basis. The policy ensured that there was no incentive at all for private holders to grow reserved species of trees, though not other species of trees. At a later stage, even other trees were considered as state property legally, but the *betta* holders could cut the grown trees after obtaining permission by paying a nominal royalty. This was done primarily to curb the temptation to make money by cutting and selling trees before they reached optimal growth.

[16] *Betta* privileges were recognised only in the case of betelnut gardens and not paddy lands. The latter were mainly in the coastal tracts, where there was not enough forest land to be assigned for all paddy cultivators. But gardens in the coastal tracts were also assigned forest land for the exercise of *betta* privileges. It is to be noted that while paddy holdings were small, gardens were much bigger.

[17] *Cf. Kanara Gazetteer*, Part II, 1883, p. 25.

Early Forest Acts and Evolution of Forest Policy

Meanwhile, the British government was arming itself with necessary legislative powers in the wake of the formation of the Forest Department, and restrictions acquired the sanction of legislation. The first legislation was the Government Forest Act, 1865, which empowered the government to declare any forest as government property. Though there was a tradition of state ownership of forests, the Act formalised this fact. But the right of the government was subject to the condition that it did not affect the existing rights and privileges enjoyed by the local community in the neighbouring forest areas.

As noted above, the process of reserving certain trees for the exclusive use of the government had started much earlier. But the concept was extended to classify forests as Reserved and Protected, and surveys and forest settlements were initiated in this direction after 1865. This led to the repeal of the earlier Act and enactment of the Indian Forest Act of 1878 which formalised this distinction and also formally recognised another category—the village forests. The new Act was more comprehensive and stringent, and further cut into the local use of forests than ever before. The government held absolute rights of ownership in reserved forests, and their products were not to be used by locals unless specifically permitted by way of grant of privilege and not as a matter of right. Access to these forests was restricted, except as thoroughfare in permitted routes. The ostensible motivation underlying the reservation of forests was to protect them against uncontrolled grazing and cultivation, and permit only a sustainable use of forests, though it did not preclude commercial use of timber in terms of scientific working plans. Protected forests were those which were yet to be surveyed and settled, but the locals' access and privileges were permitted for the time being except in those cases where they were specifically prohibited (as in the case of cutting valuable timber yielding trees). It was in the case of village forests that the rights of locals were conceded in respect of grazing, fuel needs, requirement of small wood for implements and own house construction but not for sale or barter. The extension of cultivation was possible only when permitted, and such permission was available only in areas where the exercise of local privileges was allowed, but not in the reserved forests. Because of the commercial value of timber, forests rich in timber were invariably reserved, leaving relatively less productive areas for the exercise of local use. As far as Uttara Kannada was concerned, this meant bringing the bulk of forests under the reserved category, rich as they were in timber.

The subsequent years were marked by a significant expansion of area under the reserved category. The Department was, however, transferred from the Home Secretariat to the Revenue and Agricultural Secretariat during Dufferin's viceroyalty (1884–88) in spite of the possibility of increased social discontent created by the policy, 'on the ground that the interests of agriculture were closely connected with, and in many respects even dependent on forest conservation'.[18] Working plans were also evolved to place the use of forests on a scientific basis. This led to a significant expansion and reorganisation of the Department.

There was increasing pressure on the Forest Department to raise more and more revenues and use its own revenues to meet all its needs of expansion. There was a fear that the Department would be induced to include more and more forests under the reserved category and exploit them mainly to raise revenue. From the statistics quoted by Stebbing, it is seen that as a result of the forest settlement work between 1870 and 1900, out of 117,648 sq. miles of forests in India (including Burma), 81,124 sq. miles were under the reserved category (69 per cent). Excluding Burma, the proportion amounted to 64.5 per cent, all the forests in Burma (excluding private forests and areas for which returns were not available), being closed as reserved. In Bombay Presidency, the proportion was as high as 89 per cent.[19] In the princely State of Mysore, however, the unreserved area left free for the exercise of local privileges far exceeded the reserved forest area. For the twelve Forest Divisions under the princely State, the former amounted to 22.7 lakh acres, as against 12.2 lakh acres under the latter.[20] However, this was not the pattern in British occupied India.

[18] *Cf.* E.P. Stebbing, *The forests of India*. London: John Lane and Bodley Head, 1923, Vol. II, Ch. 13, p. 456.

[19] *Ibid.*, p. 475.

[20] This is computed on the basis of data collected by Shyam Sunder and Reddy (of the Karnataka Forest Department) from the government orders issued since 1880. Their article contends that on the whole, the unreserved area exceeded the reserved which, however, could have been true only of the princely States. Even as between Uttara Kannada and Shimoga, the same difference emerges conspicuously. Taking the three Forest Divisions in Shimoga district together, the data collected by the two authors show that the reserved area accounted for 4.44 lakh acres while the unreserved area was 7.66 lakh acres. In the Honavar Division of Uttara Kannada district under the Bombay

Voelcker, therefore, tried to place the matter in a broader perspective in a well known report in 1891. He emphasised the role of agriculture and the need to make the forests meet the requirements of agriculture on a priority basis, stressing that the need to raise revenue was only next in importance.[21] The forest policy statement of 1894 showed an awareness of the need both to meet the needs of agriculture and environmental conservation. It was prepared in the light of Voelcker's Report. The policy categorised forests into: '(a) forests, the preservation of which is essential on climatic or physical grounds; (b) forests which afford a supply of valuable timbers for commercial purposes; (c) minor forests; (d) pasture lands'. The earlier classification of reserved and protected forests was not dispensed with, but could be applied to these categories. The question of restricting locals from using any of these classes was to be decided on the basis of whether the 'public benefit' from such restriction would more than outweigh the local interests. On this basis, restriction was to be almost absolute in (a) with relaxation extending as one moved towards (d). Even in regard to (b), the consideration of forest income was to be subordinated to the satisfaction of local needs. It was the less productive minor forests (c) producing inferior quality timber or only small growth of better sorts and pastures (d) which were mainly expected to meet local needs. It is worth remembering here, however, that these areas were not intrinsically less productive but could have been rendered so because of the untrammelled exercise of rights over what was regarded as common property. Thus anyone could cut timber for their own use, but its regeneration was left entirely to nature. Even in the use of (c) and (d) categories of forests, certain restrictions were put on the ground that, the 'user must not be exercised so as to annihilate its subject, and the people must be protected against their own improvidence'. Forest land could be given for cultivation, only if it did not disturb the consolidation of forest land, if cultivation was on a proper and permanent basis, and if it did not affect the forests that were either yielding good income or meeting local needs.

Presidency, the respective figures were 2.69 and 0.97 lakh acres. As we shall see from other sources also, the district as a whole also had the same pattern. See S. Shyam Sunder and A.N. Yellappa Reddy, 'Pressure on our forests', in Cecil J. Saldanha (Ed.), *Karnataka: State of environment report, 1984–85*. Bangalore, 1986, p. 13.

[21] Voelcker, *Report on the improvement of Indian agriculture*, 1891. London: Eyre and Spottiswoode, 1893, Ch. VIII.

It may be noted that the ultimate control and ownership of all classes of lands vested with the government, though in the last category (d), rights of individuals and communities could be even statutorily recognised. A lenient attitude was expressed towards the end of the policy statement, which indicated a preference for a more generous application of the forest law so that the needs of agriculture and of the local people were respected. It said:

> *The Governor-General in Council desires, therefore, that with regard both to fuel and fodder reserves and to grazing areas pure and simple, and specially to such of them as lie in the midst of cultivated tracts, it may be considered in each case whether it is necessary to class them, or, if already so classed, to retain them as forest area, and if this question is decided in the affirmative, whether it would not be better to constitute them protected rather than reserved forests.*[22]

This policy statement has to be presented in some detail here, since it continued to guide the government for a long time. It made it clear that the over-riding consideration would be 'public interest', which could well be interpreted as the interest of the larger economy; where it conflicted with local interest the latter had to be subordinated. Though this is understandable, the policy did not spell out the organisational reform needed to safeguard local interests at least where they did conflict with public interest, and to protect the environment, conserve valuable species and ensure their regeneration. It did not suggest any decentralisation of control in the form of giving over minor forests to the village or community administration at local levels, nor abrogation of the contractor system which had developed to exploit the forest (and also incidentally, both the locals and the government). While the area available for local use was on the decline, no attempts were made to raise the productivity and sustainability of whatever area remained for local use. The policy did not take into consideration the conservation and growth of forests, nor a system of incentives for the locals to grow trees and protect and develop forests. It hardly helped in making actual forest management people-oriented, and the trend towards tightening of restrictions on local use and the alienation of the local population from forest development continued.

[22] Forest Policy Circular No. 22-F, dated 19 October 1894, as reproduced in Government of Karnataka, *Background paper on forest policy,* November 1983, Mimeo, Annexure I.

The policy evolved during this period continued for a long time in all its essential detail. Even the Policy Statement of 1952 made no basic departure from it.

The Working of Forests

The *Kanara Gazetteer* has in some detail described the working of the forests then.[23] Forest officers decided what trees were to be cut, numbered and maintained a register on them along with details of their size, etc. Contractors submitted tenders to cut the trees and carry the timber to government wood stores. The superintendents of the stores further checked the quantities brought by the contractors, arranged the timber in lots, and disposed of them to dealers or private persons through auction or private sales. The role of contractors was crucial, for it was they who actually arranged to get the trees cut through labour, though supposed to be done under the supervision of the forest officials. The contractors were largely from the upper castes or communities particularly those with a trading background. They were not necessarily local, and came from neighbouring districts like Dharwad and Belgaum.

In hauling the logs to the wood stores, different techniques were employed in Uttara Kannada above and below the ghats. Above the ghats labourers from communities like Vaddars, Dheds, Marathas, Lambanis, Siddis and Muslims worked as wood-cutters and timber carriers, carrying the timber from forests and loading it on to sturdy bullock carts in teams, and taking it to wood stores. Sawing was largely manual, but the Forest Department set up steam saw-mills at Kannigeri in 1875, about eight kilometres north of Yellapur indicating the increased demand for timber and its quick processing. The mills had four plain and one cross cut saws and three engines each of twelve horsepower, and employed on an average thirty-three persons, hiring additional hands whenever there was pressure of work.[24] There were several stores up the ghats, and timber moved from here towards Belgaum, Dharwar, Hubli and other places. Roads and bridges were constructed and maintained by the Forest Department for up-country movement of forest produce.

[23] *Cf. Kanara Gazetteer*, Part I, 1883, pp. 25–32.

[24] *Ibid.*, p. 26; also Part II, p. 74.

Below the ghats, the movement was mainly along the rivers down to the wood stores established at the mouth of the rivers. Before logging, trees were usually girdled by cutting through the sap into the heart-wood, which killed the trees. They were finally cut after two or three seasons, by which time they became dry and lighter making them easy for handling. Due to the undulating terrain, elephants took on the role of bullock carts here. They not only carried the logs to the rivers, but they also guided them downstream. A single elephant could manage even a log of twenty-five to thirty-five feet long, containing fifty to eighty cubic feet of timber. Larger logs were handled by two elephants together. Elephants were owned by the contractors, but they were also available on hire. There is a graphic description in the *Kanara Gazetteer* of the operations carried out by elephants, right from the forest to the wood stores.[25] The significance of forests below the ghats, however,

[25] . . . . the elephant often works with no one on his back, and when a log gets into trouble the driver comes in front of the elephant and advises him in what they call elephant talk . . . . Up the steepest slopes and into the deepest rockiest dells the elephant unhesistantly makes his way, and tackling the largest logs, by pushing and dragging, overcomes every obstacle. Except that in dragging, a heavy hawser-like rope of green fibre is made fast to the drag holes and caught by the elephant between his teeth, he is not harnessed by the log. In moving the log he slightly raises it and draws it alongside of him, always careful to be on the upper side and to keep the log so far from him that there is no risk of its striking the feet. In this way the elephant is much safer than if he was harnessed to the log, as, if the log becomes unmanageable, he can at once let it loose. When two elephants work together, one drags and the other pushes . . . In this way the timber is dragged down the steep slopes chiefly to the Kalinadi and Gangavali rivers . . . In passing the logs down the river, the elephant is again of great use. He pushes them one by one over the shallows, keeps them straight in rapids, and shoots them along narrow channels blasted in the rock. To get water enough to float the logs through the rock cuttings the river is pounded back by a dam of stakes, leaves, grass and earth. The logs come down this reach and knock together in hopeless confusion against the dam. One elephant stands nearly up to his middle at the mouth of the rock-cut passage. Another picks his way about among the jungle of logs, takes them one by one, and turning them straight up and down the stream, passes them to the elephant at the mouth of the cut, who, with a strong push sends a log of two or three tons dancing down the channel like an oar or a walking stick. Sometimes, when the elephant at the cut is busy with a big log, a second log comes down on him from behind. When this happens he plays the second log with his hind leg with marvellous skill, stopping its force and keeping it straight till the gap is clear and he is able to pass it on. At Kadra on the Kalinadi and Gundbale on the Gangavali fifty to two hundred logs are put together and made into rafts . . . . When the rafts reach the store, elephants drag the timber above high water-mark.

Kanara Gazetteer, op. cit., Part I, pp. 28–29.

sharply declined in course of time both due to the depletion and the development of roads and railways above the ghats.

It may be noted that elephants continue to play a role in Karnataka forestry today in Shimoga and Coorg, in spite of the introduction of cranes, lorries and better roads, though not to the same extent as before. They are employed where the terrain is very undulating, to bring logs to the nearest roads. Their services in Uttara Kannada, however, have almost been discontinued due to the decline of workable forests below the ghats where elephants were in operation.

The *Kanara Gazetteer* has also recorded that during the five years ending 1882, the average yearly felling of wood in the district was 320,205 cubic feet (worth Rs. 252,030 or £ 25,203) of which 218,961 cubic feet were for export and 101,244 cubic feet for local use. The minor products (like myrobalans, soapnuts, catechu or kat, honey and wax, cinnamon, pepper and grass) yielded another Rs. 56,000. Grazing fees alone fetched Rs. 26,580 in 1882, levied on the basis of one-eighth of a rupee per head of cattle allowed in the forest. On the whole, the forests in the district yielded Rs. 144,230 in 1853–54, which increased to Rs. 410,510 in 1881–82. Expenditure increased from Rs. 56,850 to Rs. 243,870 and net profit increased from Rs. 87,380 to Rs. 166,640 during the same years.[26] Similar information was not available for Shimoga. The integration of forests with the larger economy and the inclusion of a large proportion of them under the reserved category thus proved to be financially a great success to the government even in its initial phase.

This historical stage not only saw a quantitative extension of commercialisation of forest produce, but even the negative effects of unsustainable exploitation of forests were noticed. The administrative infrastructure in the form of the Forest Department was, therefore, evolved to regulate this exploitation. The same infrastructure had to take up the unpleasant task of regulating local use as well because an untrammelled use of forest resources including forest land for cultivation was inconsistent both with the commercial use of forest resources by the larger economy and also with the long-term interests of conservation. But even in regulating the local use, the short-term local needs for fuel, fodder and timber had to be accommodated and the increasing hunger for land for cultivation could not be ignored. The Forest Department was thus saddled with the challenging task of

[26] *Ibid.*, pp. 30–31.

balancing three competing interests—short-term local needs, commercial demand, and the need to make a sustainable use of forests so that their long-term capacity to support agriculture and meet future needs of even the larger economy was not sacrificed. The British cannot be hypocritical in their interest in conservation, since they had a stake in maintaining the revenue yielding capacity of agriculture, and were aware of the role of forests in supporting agriculture. Their seriousness about scientific forest management is reflected by the fact that they conceded the inadequacy of their own expertise and welcomed German know-how. Their main drawback, however, was that their approach was purely bureaucratic and failed in enlisting local support and in evolving any dependable machinery at the local level to improve the resource base needed to support the local economy.

Chapter Four

Forest Management, Local Impact and Protests—Early Twentieth Century

Advance Towards Scientific Forestry

The period since the last decade of the nineteenth century up to about 1939 could be considered separately, though it was basically still a part of the initial stage of commercialisation. It marked a further consolidation of the integration of forests with the larger economy and their commercialisation, an advance towards scientific forestry and systematic management of forests in the interest of sustainable use, an initiation of the industrial use of forests particularly in Shimoga district, and also a sharpening of the conflicts between the locals and the government in general and the Forest Department in particular. In a sense, it marked the transition to the dominance of industrial use that was to follow after 1939 with all its consequences, and the contradictions inherent in bureaucratic forestry involving the alienation of the people came into full prominence.

Before discussing these contradictions and the protests generated, it is necessary to note how the process of scientific working of the forests was advanced. Though steps were taken towards this and even some working plans were evolved in the last quarter particularly since about 1885, they took concrete shape and were implemented on a more extensive scale only since the first decade of the present century. The working plans were formulated for each working circle and for blocks within the circles on the basis of which the trees were to be cut. On the basis of a systematic survey, the working plans actually enumerated trees to be cut in each coupe of about sixty acres—a unit for tree felling—which were thereafter given over to contractors for execution of the job. There were separate working plans for fuel growing forests and teak plantations. The working plans also involved planning of forest roads, bridges and other infrastructure.

The basic object of the working plan was well understood, even if not stated explicitly. Sometimes, it was also explicitly stated:

> *The object of the plan is to improve the jungles, and at the same time, to produce the maximum revenue* consistent with such improvement. *In other words, to realise the best possible return from the existing stock while improving it so that, in future rotations, it will yield a greater revenue.*[1] *(Emphasis added).*

Clearly, profit maximisation was not with reference to only the year concerned. An optimum rotation was decided on the basis of a comparison between the interest cost of waiting for one more year (or period) and the additional revenue expected from the growth of the tree during that period. This principle was applied to fuel wood forests also.[2]

In a mixed forest, with varying ages of trees, it meant selective felling and not clear felling. Generally, the working plans in this period at least, that is, before the stage of industrial use, envisaged selective felling though there were cases of clear felling at the level of coupes. To facilitate the growth of major and more valuable trees, improvement felling was also resorted to periodically. It involved the cutting of trees of low priority to the Department to make way for more needed trees. This meant, however, that though the reserved forests were made commercially more valuable, the biological diversity of natural forests was being eroded. It also meant that trees needed by the local people for fodder, medicine, manure, etc., received no particular attention in the promotion plan, though trees used for fuel were considered important. Plans to aid natural regeneration led to stricter regulation of grazing and measures for fire protection.

Artificial regeneration particularly of teak was also established in this period. Plantation of teak and casurina on clear felled areas began

[1] *Cf.* W.A. Miller, Deputy Conservator of Forests, 'Working Plan Report for Block VII A (between Supa and Haliyal, Kanara)', Bombay, Season 1913–14, p. 5.

[2] See, for example, W.A. Miller, Deputy Conservator of Forests, 'Working Plan for the Chandavar forests in the Western Division, Kanara, for the fuel supply of Kumta town', Bombay, Season 1913–14, 1915.

soon after the Forest Department was formally established. For example, there is a record of 73 acres of forests cleared and planted with teak in 1867–68 at Kadra and 83 acres planted with teak and sesum in Sulgeri in 1866, both in Uttara Kannada.[3] Systematic enumeration and management of these plantations to ensure their growth was, however, taken up only from around 1899 or 1900. Clearing of weeds (including bamboo, treated then as a weed obstructing teak) and thinning to reduce crop density to allow more room for the crowns to expand, was done regularly. New plantations of trees like casurina were introduced to check soil erosion on river banks in the coastal areas, which also yielded fuel. Fuel plantations were started mainly to meet the needs of government fuel depots and to bring down the pressure on forests.

Attempts were made to convert inferior forests into timber producing—particularly teak bearing—forests. The Forest Department itself resorted to burning inferior forests (after removing usable tree stock) before the onset of monsoon, sowing the area with a liberal quantity of seed immediately after the monsoon set in. Direct sowing was often preferred in the coastal tracts, and plantation over slopes. A reserve stock of one season old nursery plants was maintained in central places for planting where sowing did not yield success.[4]

A close examination of the working plans of the period reveal that the common concern was not merely with short run profit maximisation but also with the regeneration of forests. Natural regeneration was preferred and favourable conditions were created through fire protection and control of grazing. The principle that trees should be cut only after taking into account the growing stock per annum and the optimal period of cutting, which was followed in the working plans, did not of course preclude indiscriminate deforestation, since trees which had passed the point of economic optimum could be cut, and such trees constituted the bulk. The demand on forests produce was, however, still limited at least in Uttara Kannada compared to what was to follow after 1940, and forest depletion was still under check. The improved working practices in the exploitation of timber and steps taken to improve natural regeneration would also have contributed to the reversal of forest depletion in this period.

[3] R.S. Pearson, Deputy Conservator of Forests, 'Working Plan Report of the Kadra, Mardi and Sulgeri teak plantations of the Western Division, Kanara', Bombay, 1909, pp. 2–3.

[4] See, for example, S.N.J. Ratnagar, Deputy Conservator of Forests, 'Revised working plan for Ankola-Kumta, Honavar-Bhatkal, below-ghat inland forests—Kanara Southern Division', Bombay, 1929, p. 7.

Alienation of Locals and Impact on Local Economy

Such a management, however, was through a greater monopolisation of use by the State, without care for meeting local requirements. The locals could not naturally understand for whom and for what purpose the forests had to be conserved, if at all. Controls on local use were tightened as never before, cutting into customary privileges enjoyed by the locals. Though the forest policy had accepted the principle that forests should serve agriculture, this was done in a manner which the locals found frustrating. This was reflected by the fact that the area under reserved forests increased rapidly from 604 square miles (1,565 square kilometres) in 1890 to 3,015 square miles (7,811 square kilometres) in 1910 in Uttara Kannada; while protected forests where customary privileges were enjoyed almost as a matter of right dwindled into insignificance, declining from 2,835 to 132 square miles (from 7,345 to 342 square kilometres) during the same period.[5] The third category of forest areas were deemed to be non-existent in the district.[6]

The increase in reserved forests followed pressure from bureaucrats from time to time who insisted that all forests should be reserved and where necessary specified privileges could be granted to locals even in reserved forests in a way which was consistent with conservation, instead of recognising specified areas for an unregulated exercise of local privileges.[7] This was necessitated apart from the consideration of expansion of forests under government control, by the need to consolidate forest land for effective management. For example, if government forests were interspersed with cultivated gardens and village forests, it hampered the machinery to guard forests against free grazing, theft and fire. But this conflicted seriously with local interests. The reserved forests extended right up to the doorstep in many settlements; so jealous was the Forest Department to safeguard its own rights in these forests, that from 1902 to 1904 the locals were prohibited

[5] Quoted in the Representation made by M.D. Karki to Governor of Bombay, in *KV*, 11 March 1920. The total forest area in 1880 was 9,189 sq. kms according to the *Kanara Gazetter*.

[6] Collins report says, 'Village Forest under Section 27 of the Indian Forest Act . . . does not as yet exist in Kanara'. *Cf.* G.F.S. Collins, 'A history of forest settlement work in Kanara', Poona, 1923, p. 1.

[7] This is apparent from Collin's account, *ibid.*, p. 1.

from collecting even dry leaves from areas for manure.[8] *Betta* land was limited to four acres for each acre of garden in below-ghat areas in 1908, though nine acres of *betta* was allowed per acre of garden in up-ghat areas. Supply of green manure, fodder, stakes for fences and wood for implements for agriculture became scarce, as this supply was dependent on a free access to forests. Grazing areas were further restricted and a fee of one-eighth of a rupee was charged per head of cattle in permitted areas. There were complaints that areas where grazing was permitted were very poor in grass. The forest personnel could impound animals for trespass, and penalise villagers for alleged theft of forest produce and for starting a fire. This gave immense scope for friction as well as bribery. They were empowered to levy collective fines on villagers when a forest caught fire, even after receiving their help in putting out the fire. The locals also complained of increased hazards of wild animals attacking cattle and crops, and the menace of malaria causing mosquitoes, since the buffer between forests and settlements disappeared.

Though the government had opened fuel depots in towns and villages, there was a ban on the collection of fuel wood from forests in areas served by these depots. This put the rural poor to great difficulties, because they had now to pay for it (even if less than in the open market) while they used to get it free earlier. Moreover, since depot prices were lower, contractors were not motivated to supply wood to depots resulting in a short supply. In an interesting letter to the Editor, a poor 'Sansari' (family man) had complained that through hard wage labour he could somehow buy rice and salt to avert starvation for his family, but that they might nevertheless have to face it due to fuel wood not being available for cooking even in a forest district like Kanara. The Forest Department had granted him neither the necessary access to the forest nor enough fuel through its depots, he explained.[9]

All these restrictions not only had the effect of reversing the extension of cultivated area at the expense of forests, they also seemed to have led to a decline. This is evident from the representations made by the local agriculturists' associations to the government. From the figures quoted in these representations[10] (which in turn were based on

[8] *Cf.* G.R. Masur, 'Forest grievances in North Kanara', Pamphlet No. 1, Kumta, 1927, p. 2.

[9] See *KV*, 9 June 1921, p. 3.

[10] See, for example, G.R. Masur, 'Representation to the Collector of Kanara on behalf of agricultural association', Kumta, dated 12.3.1918; also M.D. Karki et al., 'Memorial on behalf of agriculturists and land owners of Kanara to Revenue Ministry', Bombay, 1938.

official statistics), net cultivated area appears to have declined in Uttara Kannada from 240 thousand acres in 1890–91 to 211 thousand acres in 1914–15. While the area under rice declined from 196 thousand acres to 173 thousand acres in the same period, and further to 154 thousand acres in 1933–34. Garden land also declined from 23.3 to 20.7 and further to 17.3 thousand acres during the same period. Similar decline was reported in the case of sugarcane and ragi. Area under a second crop, usually for cultivation of pulses, after the harvesting of rainfed rice, was also reported to have declined due to the shortage of fencing material. Restrictions on the collection of forest produce, grazing and cumri cultivation and the advance of forests right up to settlements were pointed out as some of the reasons for the decline in both cultivated area and in the population itself, indicating a deterioration in the living conditions.

Table 4.1 Growth of Population 1901–41

	Population (in hundred thousand)			*Rate of Growth in the Decade*		
Year	*N K*	*Shimoga*	*India**	*N K*	*Shimoga*	*India**
1901	4.54	5.32	2384.0	—	—	—
1911	4.31	5.17	2520.9	−5.0	−2.8	5.7
1921	4.02	4.93	2513.2	−6.7	−4.6	−0.3
1931	4.18	5.20	2789.8	4.0	5.5	11.0
1941	4.41	5.51	3186.6	5.5	6.0	14.2

N K North Kanara (Uttara Kannada).
* Adjusted for the present territory of India.
Source: M.V. Nadkarni and M. Johnson Samuel, 'Population and workforce changes in a forest region', *Social Science Probings*, Vol. I (3), September 1984; based in turn on various volumes of the Population Census of India.

Population in the district declined more sharply in the district than in the country as a whole, and increased only marginally when the rate of growth was much higher in the country. This can be seen from Table 4.1. The decline in population was confined mostly to the upghat region in Uttara Kannada and many labourers and *cumri* cultivators migrated from the district, and educated migrants gave up their lands and sought office jobs.

It may be noted here that the Malnad region, particularly Uttara Kannada, was considered to be malaria infested, which affected the availability of labour for cultivation and gardening and increased the costs. This could have been another factor underlying the decline in both cultivated area and population. But this was not necessarily an independent or exogenous factor. The locals attributed the increasing malaria menace directly to the increasing area under reserved forests and government's apathy in tackling the disease.

Protest Movements and their Class Base

The alienation of the locals from forest use and the consequent discontent was by no means unique to Uttara Kannada. Apart from a similar phenomenon among the tribals in Thana district mentioned earlier, there is a prolonged history of unrest and protests among the peasants of the Himalayan region in Uttar Pradesh.[11] There have been several other instances as were in the old Madras Presidency, Travancore State and Midnapur district of Bengal.[12] Such discontent cut across all classes of the local population dependent on forests for subsistence. However, the opposition to State forestry was said to be far more intense among lower castes and tribals,[13] which was not true of Uttara Kannada.

In this district too a sense of alienation and grievance had affected all sections of the local population, yet the local elite were the most aggrieved and vocal. There was no conflict of interests between landlords, tenants and labourers as far as the Forest Department and forest issues were concerned. The elite in this region consisted of landlords, gardeners (owners of betelnut and pepper plantations) and merchants. Restrictions on encroachment of forests for the extension of cultivation and on grazing had directly affected the landlords and gardeners, while restrictions on the extractions of timber, fuel wood and other forest produce affected the merchants. For similar reasons, tenants, who were in the middle of the social and agrarian hierarchy, were also affected. Restrictions on grazing and fuel wood extraction affected all

[11] See Ramachandra Guha, Forestry and social protest in British Kumaun, c. 1893–1921, in Ranjit Guha (Ed.), *Subaltern studies IV*. New Delhi, 1985.

[12] Ramachandra Guha and Madhav Gadgil, 'State forestry and social conflict in British India: A study in the ecological bases of agrarian protest', Technical Report No. 51, Centre for Ecological Sciences, Indian Institute of Science, Bangalore, January 1988.

[13] *Ibid.*, p. 25.

sections, including the rural poor. An increase in revenue assessment as a result of the Revision Settlement of 1914–15,[14] infuriated the landlords and gardeners, adding to their grievances. To the locals,

> *the Government was only an expropriator, coming only to collect the taxes and land revenue, but incapable of assuring them any protection. Even when their betelnut plantations failed to yield due to plant diseases, or other reasons, tax had to be paid and all demands for concessions had fallen on deaf ears. The plantation owners living in secluded hilly tracts had no protection against armed gangs of robbers.*[15]

Though all sections had grievances, a free local use of forests had benefited different sections of the local population to different degrees. Landlords, gardeners and merchants had extracted the lion's share of benefits from the forests mainly for profit, though the dependence of the other sections was mainly for subsistence. It is not surprising, therefore, that the classes which dominated local agriculture also were in the forefront of the protest movements. They were shrewd enough to take along the tenants and the landless and to raise issues which interested and involved them.

There has been a long history of sporadic uprisings by peasants of Uttara Kannada against the British ever since 1800.[16] Apart from forest issues, there were other grievances as well. Insistence on payment of taxes even in years of yield failure has already been discussed. Salt regulations had also affected the livelihood of salt-pan workers.[17] Apathy towards developing Karwar port and a railway line in the district had affected the merchant class.[18] But it was the forest issue which had aroused the majority of the people on a sustained and organised basis.

One of the earliest expressions of organised protests against forest administration was the convening of the Kaanadā Vanadukha Nivarini Sabhā (Kanara Conference on Forest Grievances) in 1884 in Sirsi. By then, the impact of the Indian Forest Act of 1878 had been fully felt in the district following the extension of reserved forests. The next

[14] See G.S. Halappa, *History of freedom movement in Karnataka, Bangalore, Government of Mysore, 1964, Vol. II, p. 110.*

[15] *See Suryanath Kamath (Ed.), Uttara Kannada District Gazetteer,* Government of Karnataka, 1985, p. 164.

[16] *Ibid.*, pp. 162–87

[17] *Ibid.*, p. 165.

[18] *Ibid.*, p. 164.

meeting took place again at Sirsi in 1887 which deputed a local leader from the landlord-merchant class to the Indian National Congress to be held in Madras the same year. There is a record of such conferences on forest grievances being held again in 1916 and 1917 at Bilgi in Uttara Kannada.[19] Two periodicals—*Kaanadā Vritta* launched in 1916 at Karwar and *Kaanadā Dhureena* in 1917 at Kumta—were extremely useful in ventilating local grievances and played a prominent role in forming public opinion in favour of anti-British movements including the National Freedom Movement in the 1920s and later in Uttara Kannada.[20] Agriculturists' associations and leading landlords and gardeners gave the needed organisational support to the protest movements and to the two periodicals. They also made representations to the government from time to time, demanding an extension of privileges in forest areas and relaxation of restrictions. These associations were particularly active in the coastal areas and the area around Sirsi.

The mood in the country at this time was increasingly in favour of civil disobedience which affected Uttara Kannada also. It was felt that mere representations would yield little. The district was very responsive to any call from the Indian National Congress, and the local newspapers gave wide coverage and support to the freedom movement under the Congress Party. It was readily recognised by the British that local discontent with the Forest Laws could be used by the landlords to incite disobedience and that the district could be in the forefront of the movement.[21] The British policy was to forbid public speeches which could incite people to break laws, to award stringent punishments and fines (including group or community fines), and at the same time to give concessions and relax restrictions wherever it suited the government so that public resentment would not get out of control. Concessions began to be given right from the 1920s, though the firm grip which the Forest Department had already established over forests

[19] *Ibid.*, p. 165.

[20] *Ibid.*, p. 165.

[21] A letter from the Commissioner of the Southern Division to the Collector of Karwar, dated 7.1.1922, states:

> . . . . If Civil Disobedience is started anywhere in the Southern Division it will be in Kanara . . . . a probable form of it would be the incitement of lower castes to break the Forest Laws. Any refusal to pay land revenue would involve the risk to the well-to-do of the loss of their lands, which they are not likely to incur.

See Halappa, *op. cit.*, p. 112.

was never loosened. As such, protest movements continued in spite of concessions and accommodation.

Concessions and Accommodation

The first step in this process of limited liberalisation was taken in 1920 by permitting a free supply of bamboo for fencing, transfer of 'bettas' to the Revenue Department, extension of minor forests, and a reduction in the number of reserved trees from twenty-five to seven[22] (raised subsequently to fifteen). G.F.S. Collins, as a forest settlement officer, recommended restoration of some of the customary privileges in 1921 and in the coastal areas of Uttara Kannada. His proposal involved mainly an extension of the area under minor forests to meet the needs of agriculture and to raise fuel wood to feed depots. More areas were 'opened' for the exercise of local privileges. Closure of blocks or coupes for the exercise of fuel privileges was to be decided on the basis of both the supply position in depots and the condition of forests. However, where forests were considered as damaged by the exercise of privileges, they were to be closed and expenditure for repairing the damage could be recovered from the people. The privilege of cutting green leaves for manure was, however, extended to all open areas, and not restricted to certain areas among them. The proposal also included permission to convert areas of minor forests permanently for cultivation. This was done since minor forests were not viewed as net revenue yielding and relieved the Forest Department of expenditure on guarding them.[23]

These concessions were considered to be highly inadequate and a series of lengthy editorials criticising the forest policy appeared in *KV* in 1923. Further representations were made by leaders. More concessions were demanded in *betta* lands in up-ghats areas, particularly the right to have stone-and-mud walls around them and the right over more trees in *bettas*, apart from the customary privileges of grazing and green leaves from such areas. There was a demand for more land for grazing for those who did not have *bettas*.

[22] Press Note by Government of Bombay, 21 September 1920.

[23] G.F.S. Collins, 'Modifications in forest settlement of Kanara coastal tract', Karwar, 1921. Also Collins, 1923, *op. cit*.

A forest committee consisting both of official and non-official members was appointed in 1925 to examine forest grievances. Though its opinion was divided between official and non-official representatives, the government announced further concessions in 1927. Some of these concessions were: a buffer zone of clear area extending from village settlements up to a quarter mile was permitted; trees in grasslands would not be assigned to contractors; stumps and other timber left by contractors could be extracted by villagers; fuel needed for preparing jaggery (gur) out of sugarcane was to be provided free by the department; contractors were asked not to obstruct villagers from cutting brushwood and other permitted varieties; fees for grazing, collecting fuel and green leaves, etc., were reduced; thorny bushes, etc., were permitted to be burnt in minor forests to allow better growth of grass and eliminate shelter for wild animals; villagers' right to graze their cattle in traditional grazing areas within their village was recognised. Total grazing land in the district was also proposed to be increased on the basis of three acres per head of cattle, taking the district as a whole as the unit for calculation. But no village could have a right to grazing land on the basis of its cattle population.[24] It was permitted wherever it suited the convenience of the Forest Department, and these areas were generally reported to be areas of poor growth of grass. No systematic management of grazing lands from the perspective of stepping up the yield of fodder was envisaged.

Even as these concessions were being announced in the district, an important legislation was passed at the national level, the Indian Forest Act of 1927. Its significance lies in the fact that it has not yet been replaced, though it has been amended. Following independence, the States enacted their own Acts for subjects under their jurisdiction consistent with the provisions of this Act. Though the Act continued the earlier classification of reserved, protected and village forests, it gave more powers to the government in the reserved forests, increased the number of listed offences and enhanced the punishment for some of these offences. However, no control or regulation was envisaged for village forests. Though such forests were deemed to be non-existent in Uttara Kannada, the locals enjoyed free access to minor forests. In the case of 'protected' forests, rights and privileges of 'persons' were recorded which the government had no powers to reduce. The emphasis in the Act was more on the rights and privileges of individuals

[24] *Cf. KV*, 8 August 1927.

rather than local communities, which was intended to assuage the local elite resulting in the sanctification of institutions like *bettas*. This was not unique to Uttara Kannada, as similar privileges of individual cultivators were recognised in other areas too—bettas and occupied '*kans*' (evergreen forests) in Shimoga and other Western Ghat districts of old Mysore, *kumaki* lands and 'assessed kans' in Dakshina Kannada (South Kanara), and *bané* lands in Coorg.[25] The Act brought no particular relief and the local discontent continued in Uttara Kannada.

Meanwhile the freedom movement under the Congress had gathered tremendous momentum, and inspired more and more people in Uttara Kannada to civil disobedience and satyagraha. The Salt Satyagraha in Ankola in April 1930 was a tremendous success in spreading the nationalist cause,[26] and the people of Sirsi-Siddapur region, the traditional base for forest grievances, could not fall far behind in launching another satyagraha in the district, this time on forest issues.

> *It was started on the 4th of August (1930) . . . . As the procession went on, people in hundreds came from the villages and joined it; so that when it reached the forest, there was a multitude which staggered the authorities who had gone to put down the Satyagraha. Sandal trees were cut down, the wood was loaded in carts, and everyone carried branches, the return procession giving the appearance of a moving forest. The wood was brought to Sirsi and auctioned off . . . . Every village in the taluks of Sirsi and Siddapur followed this example . . . . The Government . . . . began to arrest the Satyagrahis who had come from outside and a few important local leaders. The latter awakened the women to action . . . . The jungle Satyagraha could not be put down by force, for the people of whole villages would move out in thousands and would vie with one another in getting arrested.*[27]

No-tax campaign was launched subsequently (1930–31) in the district, in Ankola and Sirsi-Siddapur regions. Searches and forcible seizures of property were carried out to harass people. No buyers came forward to bid when seized property was tried to be auctioned.[28] These satyagrahas and campaigns were supported by all communities and classes in the district, including women.

[25] For details, see Government of Karnataka, *Background paper on forest policy*. Prepared for the Economic and Planning Council, Department of Forests, November 1983, Annexure XIII.

[26] See Halappa, *op. cit.*, pp. 175–79.

[27] *Ibid.*, p. 183.

[28] *Ibid.*, pp. 189–90.

Even while people were staging demonstrations and offering satyagraha, the authorities began to realise that merely bureaucratic and oppressive measures would not be effective, and efforts were made to involve popular representatives in advisory bodies to guide the local forest administration in forest management. A Forest Advisory Committee was formed in 1928 in Uttara Kannada, consisting of both official and non-official members. But the locals could not be bought over by such measures. Their strategy was to use these opportunities to voice their grievances without abandoning their plans of offering resistance through satyagraha. The Conservator of Forests, Bombay, gave expression to official frustration with the working of these committees thus: 'the present forest advisory committees which are semi-official bodies, are concerned more or less with forest grievances of the people and do no constructive work'. He proposed, therefore, the constitution of non-official forest associations (like the Tree Association in America) whose object was to impress on the public the role of forests in maintaining environmental balance and increasing the economic resources of the country, and to bring about a better understanding between the people and the government in forest matters The government, however, did not dissolve the Advisory Committees then, but asked them to undertake the work expected of a Forest Association.[29] These committees continued to function till 1942 when they were dissolved.

These committees seem to have succeeded in extracting some concessions from time to time from the government. Since teak plantations near village settlements were a source of friction and interfered with the exercise of local privileges, it was decided in 1938 not to raise new teak plantations within half a mile of the village site in teak areas and a mile from the same in non-teak areas. Forests could be cleared in non-teak areas up to half a mile around 'substantial villages' (those with 20 acres of garden or 100 acres of rice land), but in teak areas up to only a furlong. *Cumri* cultivation was allowed in the strip area for the first two years only after its clearance. There was some demand for planting eucalyptus trees in the strip area because of the belief that they acted as mosquito repellents. Not only were the farmers allowed to plant them in the strip areas, the Forest Department was instructed to supply the needed seedlings. The normal period of closure of

[29] As quoted in the Government Resolution No. 4789/33 signed by M.J. Desai, Deputy Secretary to Government, Revenue Department, Bombay, dated 22 August 1938.

forests under regeneration was limited to 5 years, after which permitted privileges could be exercised. Cane and grass used for making baskets, brooms, etc., were also allowed free to villages for domestic use and for cottage industries, but not for direct sale or barter. Carts were allowed on permitted forest tracts, but only to lift earth, stone and fallen leaves, and not small wood—the latter allowed only as head-loads.[30]

In 1942, the Forest Advisory Committees were dissolved and their functions were transferred to Special Sub-committees of the District Rural Development Boards. This seems to have reduced their importance and authority somewhat. Moreover, far-reaching changes which were introduced since 1939 marked the beginning of the Second World War and the acceleration of industrial use of forest produce. These changes drowned the local voice on forest matters for a long time.

Much that was done by way of systematic management was to be undone after 1939, not by the local people but by the government itself. During the early part of the century, only the government seemed to be concerned with conservation and environmental protection provided by the forests. Though commercial exploitation had already begun on a significant scale, it was realised that it could be carried out only through a systematic management of forests that conserved forests at the same time, so that long-term returns from forests were not sacrificed. The local people hardly felt it necessary to press the issue of conservation for it had not hit them from that direction, and did not think of their own use of forests as a possible threat in any way to conservation of forests or their environmental role. Moreover, deforestation had not arisen yet as a conspicuous phenomenon. During the phase of the dominance of industrial use, however, the larger economy became the major agent of deforestation, and made the local people take up the environmental issue. The conflicts with the local people took on a new context and perspective.

[30] *Cf.* Government of Bombay, Revenue Department, Resolutions No. 3449/33, dated 24.2.1938; No. 8791/33, dated 25.11.1939.

Chapter Five

Dominance of Industrial Use

Forest Using Industries

Though dominance of the larger economy in the use of forest resources was firmly established by the early part of the twentieth century, there was a major technical change in the use of forest resources when forest produce was processed for modern industries like plywood and paper and pulp mills. Using modern saw-mills for cutting timber was started by the end of the nineteenth century in Uttara Kannada as noted earlier. Several more such mills were set up both in Uttara Kannada and Shimoga by 1939. But the use of forest produce took a quantum leap thanks to the spur to industrialisation given under state auspices by Visvesvarayya.

The Mysore Iron and Steel Works (MISW), a government owned company initiated in Shimoga as early as 1918, was designed to produce industrial chemicals (calcium acetate, methanol and wood tars) out of wood, yielding charcoal as a by-product which was to be used in place of coke in the production of pig iron. When the plant was designed, charcoal produced pig iron was considered superior, but a technological breakthrough in the 1920s improved the quality of coke produced pig iron. Moreover, synthetic and cheaper methods of producing these industrial chemicals were also developed. To add to this, prices of pig iron collapsed, and MISW's future was endangered.[1] It has survived to date, however. But it emerged as a major consumer of forest resources, particularly fuel wood. Even in its initial stage, its consumption of wood was about 120 thousand tonnes in 1923.

The other major unit was the Mysore Match Manufacturing Company,

[1] See George Baldwin, *Industrial growth in South India—Case study in economic development*. Illinois: The Free Press, 1959, esp. p. 69.

which was started as a private company in 1927, and taken over by the government in 1939–40. The Mysore Paper Mills, a government owned enterprise, began operation at Bhadravati in 1939. The government also set up a sandalwood oil factory at Shimoga in 1944. Several units were set up in the small sector which consumed softwood or timber. This included a match factory, handmade paper units, a plywood factory (at Talguppa) and nearly twenty-nine saw-mills. To meet the increasing demand for industrial charcoal both from MISW and outside the district, nearly seven distillation units were established in the early seventies with a capacity of producing two to four tonnes of charcoal a day. They have been expected to use only waste wood.[2]

After the first modern saw-mill was set up by the Forest Department in Uttara Kannada in 1875, another one was set up in the coastal town of Kumta by a private party in 1907. This was followed by a long gap. When the demand for timber rose sharply in the wake of the Second World War, the government sponsored a saw-mill in the private sector at Kirwatti in 1942, and set up another modern mill at Dandeli in 1943. By the mid-seventies, there were approximately fifty saw-mills (including unregistered ones) in the district, started by timber merchants and contractors—partly local and partly from outside, particularly from Hubli, Dharwar and Belgaum. The forests of the district attracted the business houses of north India, particularly Marwari capital. Both the Indian Plywood Manufacturing Company (1944) and the West Coast Paper Mill (1955) were established in the private sector at Dandeli. Harihar Polifibres, a Birla concern, set up in the neighbouring Dharwar district in 1972, also depended on the forests of Uttara Kannada and Shimoga. The major consumers of timber and pulpwood in Uttara Kannada were all in the private sector, unlike Shimoga where state owned mills played a major role in this respect.

These major industries in the private sector were encouraged by the government, particularly after the Reorganisation of States. At the time of their establishment, these industries usually entered into an agreement with the government, whereby the Forest Department had to supply raw material for agreed periods—extending from five to thirty years at a stretch—and agreed prices. These prices were far below the market prices and the replacement cost of wood consumed. Since the industry was getting raw material like bamboo at such low

[2] *Cf.* Government of Karnataka, *Gazetteer of Shimoga District*, 1975, Chapter V, pp. 170–71, 185–201.

prices, it had no interest in their regeneration.[3] The management of resource supply was such that there was a dichotomy between resource use and resource regeneration, the user having little responsibility for regeneration. The Forest Department was under constant pressure to make available forest produce to support the drive for industrialisation. The principles of forest management that were followed rather strictly particularly since the 1890s had to be compromised, not because of a voluntary option exercised by the Forest Department as such, but because of the growing pressures from the larger economy with which the forest region was more closely integrated than ever before.

National Forest Policy

There was an awareness of the conflicting demands on the forests and the need to reconcile them in broader and long-term interests. A new National Forest Policy was adopted[4] in 1952 which reiterated the basic principles and concepts of the earlier policy of 1894 and recognised six paramount needs of the country: a balanced and complementary land use; checking floods and soil erosion; establishing tree lands or afforestation for larger environmental care and well being of people; meeting local needs for firewood and for agriculture; the needs of defence, communications and industry; the need for maximum revenue consistent with other needs above. These needs were taken as indicative of the diverse functions of forests.

The policy, therefore, classified forests into four categories according to their specific functions: (a) protection forests which were meant to be preserved in broader environmental interests; (b) national forests to meet the needs of industry, defence and communications; (c) village forests to meet local needs; and (d) tree lands, which were outside the scope of normal forest management but essential for the amelioration of physical conditions of the country, such as to prevent flooding and soil erosion.

[3] See Madhav Gadgil, S.N. Prasad and Rauf Ali, 'Forest management in India—A critical review', Indian Institute of Science, Bangalore, 1982, Mimeo, p. 48.

[4] See *National Forest Policy*, Lok Sabha Secretariat, New Delhi, 1985, Appendix 2, pp. 55–67.

The functional classification was not meant to replace the earlier classification in terms of the 1927 Act which was based on the degree of control exercisable on them. The functional classification of 1952 had no legal significance, and was not considered mutually exclusive. Apparently, its main objective was to identify the forest areas which were to serve specific functions, though there was no clear indication of the weightage or priority assigned to different functions, unless it is presumed that the order in which the forests were classified itself indicated the priority. There was also not much evidence of whether certain forest areas were recognised specifically as environmentally sensitive and as out of bounds for commercial exploitation or for take over for developmental purposes of the larger economy.

The policy, however, made it absolutely clear that the interests of the larger economy shall prevail over local interests. It said,

> *The accident of a village being situated close to a forest does not prejudice the right of the country as a whole to receive the benefits of a national asset . . . . While, therefore, the needs of the local population must be met to a reasonable extent, national interests should not be sacrificed because they are not directly discernible, nor should the rights and interests of future generations be subordinated to the improvidence of the present generation.*[5]

Though this passage indicates that local interests had to be subordinated to the need for environmental protection in larger national interests, the actual practice showed that larger national interests meant maximising economic growth.

The recommendations of the National Commission on Agriculture also did not go much further. The Commission sought to resolve the problem of multiple roles of forests on the same lines, that is, by reclassifying forest areas purposewise as follows: (a) protection forests, (b) production forests, and (c) social forests.

> *Forests managed primarily for protection occupy hill slopes, watershed of rivers, river banks, sea shores and other localities vulnerable to erosion and degradation . . . . Production forests which are commercial forests, should comprise valuable or potentially valuable timber bearing stands* occurring in favourable regions *which are indispensable for development of the country and for meeting diverse requirements of the national economy . . . . The social forests should cover waste lands, panchayat lands, village common*

[5] *Ibid.*, p. 57.

lands on the side of roads, canal banks and railway lines, which may be brought under forest plantations, shelter belts and mixed forestry comprising raising of grass and leaf fodder, fruit trees and fuel wood trees.[6]

Unfortunately, even this classification could not go far enough. The reason being that the 'favourable regions' which provide the base for production forestry are also the areas which need protection, occurring as they do on hill slopes, watersheds, etc. It is these areas which are rich in forest wealth and have great potential for meeting the energy and raw material needs, and yet are ecologically sensitive. The governments—both the colonial and the present—found the temptation of using them for commercial purposes too strong and have exploited the forests, often to the detriment of both environmental and local interests. The period following 1939 saw unprecedented demands both on forest area and produce in the country as a whole. The Western Ghats and Karnataka were no exception.

Demands of Larger Economy on Forest Area

To be fair, the demand from the paper and pulp industry was only a part of the demand from the larger economy. The tremendous spread of electrification in the fifties and the sixties created a massive demand for wooden poles for fixing wires and street lighting in towns and cities. However, once it was realised that timber could not meet this demand iron poles were used (now cement poles have taken their place). The price extracted from forests by electricity needed by the larger economy was, however, far heavier in terms of forest area submerged by hydroelectric projects and also the area needed for the resettlement of displaced people, particularly in Uttara Kannada and Shimoga districts. For example, 2,338 hectares were released in Shimoga district in 1964 to resettle people displaced by the Sharavathi project alone. What is worse, as pointed out by Shyam Sunder and Yellappa Reddy, such areas are not in one block. 'The release covered a total number of 189 blocks, honey combing the entire forest belt. Today the extent covered under agriculture by these people is 5,443 ha'.[7]

[6] Government of India, *Report of the National Commission on Agriculture*, Part IX, Forestry, 1976, pp. 24–25 (emphasis added).

[7] Shyam Sunder and Yellappa Reddy, *op. cit.* (see fn 20 in Ch. 3), p. 17.

According to official sources, the decline in the area under forests (as per legal status, not necessarily under forest cover) in Karnataka between 1956 and 1981 was as shown in Table 5.1. It is interesting to see from the table that while the extension of cultivation, an important form of local use of the forest area, continued to be significant during this phase, accounting for over 30 per cent of the decline in area, the other demands on the forest area from the larger economy were overwhelmingly large (nearly 70 per cent). Hydroelectric projects alone accounted for about 48 per cent of the decline, directly and indirectly.

Table 5.1 Forest Area Lost Since 1956 in Karnataka (Purpose-wise)

Purpose	*Area Lost in Hectares*	*Per cent to Total Area Lost*
1. Hydroelectric projects (Kali, Chakra, Varahi, Gangavati and Bedthi Phase I)	41,068	18.4
2. Direct submersion	35,840	16.1
3. Rehabilitation of the displaced	25.820	11.6
4. Power lines	1,688	0.8
5. Colony, roads and townships	2.121	0.9
6. Mining	42,676	19.2
7. Other non-agricultural use	6,297	2.8
8. Extension of cultivation	67,217	30.2
	222,727	100

Source: Suryanath Kamath (Ed.), *Karnataka State Gazetteer*, Part I. Government of Karnataka, 1982, p. 130.

In the meantime, forest area (legally defined) is reported to have increased in the state from 2,600 to 3,840 thousand hectares on the whole in spite of the decline in the area noted earlier. The increase was due mainly to the transfer of uncultivated revenue lands to the Forest Department for purposes of afforestation. It should be noted, however, that while additions made to the forest area had hardly any tree wealth, the area lost—particularly in Uttara Kannada—comprised rich forests. Of the 223 thousand hectares of forest area lost since 1956, this district alone accounted for 84 thousand hectares.[8]

[8] This is as per statistics obtained from the Kanara Circle of the Forest Department with its head office at Dharwad. Of the 84 thousand hectares, 21 thousand acres were lost due to the extension of cultivation.

Simultaneously with the initiation of development projects, both Uttara Kannada and Shimoga underwent a qualitative transformation, which resulted in a reversal of the earlier behaviour of population growth. Improved infrastructural facilities and eradication of malarial conditions in the region were the primary contributory factors underlying this reversal. As a result, population began to grow in both districts at a higher rate than in the country as a whole, the difference being particularly conspicuous between 1951 and 1961. Significant immigration took place during this decade, which was both on account of new industrial units and the settlement of refugees and displaced persons. The population changes can be seen from Table 5.2, which can be compared with Table 4.1.

Table 5.2 Growth of Population after 1941

	Population (in hundred thousand)			*Rate of Growth in the Decade (per cent)*		
Year	*N K*	*Shimoga*	*India**	*N K*	*Shimoga*	*India**
1951	5.18	6.63	3610.9	17.4	20.3	13.3
1961	6.90	10.17	4392.3	33.2	53.4	21.6
1971	8.49	13.01	5481.6	23.0	27.9	24.8
1981	10.71	16.58	6851.8	26.2	27.4	25.0

Note: Comparable with figures in Table 4.1.
Source: M.V. Nadkarni and M. Johnson Samuel, 'Population and workforce changes in a forest region', *Social Science Probings*, Vol. I (3), September 1984; based in turn on various volumes of the Population Census of India.

It may be noted that even as late as 1987, the density of population in both the districts was lower than in the country as a whole, being 104 per sq. km in Uttara Kannada and 157 in Shimoga, compared to the country's average of 221. The population increase during the seventies was a reflection of the increased level of integration of the region with the larger economy. While pressure on land for the extension of cultivation is not unimportant still, the other sources of pressure coming from the larger economy were the major factor underlying the pressure on forests in this region (see footnote 5 here).

Denudation and Official Reaction

More poignant than the decline in the size of forest area legally so defined, has been its degradation and denudation. This damage has been much greater. Of the 3.84 million hectares of legally defined forest area in 1981–82 in Karnataka, the area with adequate stock was estimated to be only 1.35 million hectares (i.e., 35 per cent). Of the rest, 1.14 million hectares were practically unwooded, and 1.35 million hectares considered degraded.[9] In 1980–81 in the country as a whole, though 67.4 million hectares were reported to be under forests as per land use statistics, only 46 million hectares were actually under tree cover (68 per cent). This shows that the situation in Karnataka has been probably much worse.

The two districts being studied here have also been very much a part of the same process, as seen from the official data. Table 5.3 presents the proportion of denuded forest area to total forest area by

Table 5.3 Proportion of Denuded Forest Area by Category of Forests in Uttara Kannada and Shimoga Districts

(per cent to total forest area under respective categories)

Category of Forests	*Uttara Kannada*		*Shimoga*	
	1960	*1980*	*1960*	*1980*
1. Reserved forests	2.9	18.7	10.8	41.4
2. District forests (protected, unreserved)	—	—	31.8	65.6
3. Minor forests	46.3	95.4	25.6	96.5
4. *Betta* lands (under private privileges)	51.0	81.4	44.8	90.3
5. All categories	14.1	37.2	20.1	58.0
Area with good forests (all) as per cent of total geographical area	70.4	51.4	27.4	16.4
Denuded forest area (all) as per cent of total geographical area	11.6	30.5	6.9	22.6

Source: Based on Shyam Sunder and Yellappa Reddy, *op. cit.*, Tables III and IV, p. 16; based in turn on the working plan records of the Forest Department.

categories of forests, as also on the whole taking all categories together. The area with adequate forest cover as per cent of total geographical

[9] See government of Karnataka, *Background paper on forest policy*, Department of Forests, November 1983, Annexure IV, pp. iv-1.

area declined within the two decades of the sixties and the seventies from 70.4 to 51.4 in Uttara Kannada and from 27.4 to 16.4 in Shimoga. Interestingly, the process of denudation was quicker in the unreserved forest area left relatively free for the exercise of community and private privileges in both the districts. The level of denudation was higher in these forests than in the reserved forests in 1960, but the gap widened considerably by 1980. Even the bettas and benas which are subject to the exclusive privileges have been denuded much faster than the reserved forests. Private exclusive privileges have not necessarily played a preservative role. The level of denudation in these areas was actually higher than in the other unreserved forests in 1960, but by 1980 minor forests, where community privileges are freely exercised, were more denuded than the bettas. The reservation of forests has to some extent checked the process of denudation by making the process slower than in the unreserved areas, but this is a matter of little consolation since even in the reserved forests, it has been significant enough especially in Shimoga.

The denudation of unreserved forests has adversely affected the local needs. On the one hand, the requirement of firewood needs has been increasing sharply; on the other hand, the area available to satisfy this requirement declined rapidly. This is clearly illustrated by Table 5.4. It may be noted that the decline in area is not merely quantitative,

Table 5.4 Requirement of Firewood as Against the Status of Area Earmarked to Satisfy the Same

Name of the Town (in Uttara Kannada)	*Requirement of Firewood (tons)*		*Area Earmarked from Minor Forests in Hectares*	
	1926	*1984*	*1926 (Productive)*	*1984 (Unproductive)*
Ankola and Gokarn	300	5900	4258	3800
Honnavar	800	4825	1977	1500
Bhatkal	1000	7468	2357	2160
Kumta	1200	5300	6125	5320

Source: Shyam Sunder and Yellappa Reddy, *op. cit.*, Table II, p. 15.

but also qualitative. These minor forests were considered productive in 1926, but unproductive in 1984, due to the near total denudation. Here also, even more than in the case of industrial use of forest produce, there was dichotomy between resource use and resource regeneration, the user having little responsibility for regeneration. No institutional framework had been evolved even in this phase of economic development when institution building as part of planned development had been undertaken on a massive scale in other spheres of the economy.

The easy approach to meet the crisis was through a liberalisation of local access to both reserved and unreserved forests, in practice if not officially. Though officially villagers are allowed to remove only headloads of dead firewood from reserved forests, it is not difficult to find caravans of people, each person carrying a headload of wood till the outskirts of the forests and then transporting it on donkeys, carts and even trains. Such unofficial exploitation is not all for subsistence, but for sale too mostly in the local markets. The local forest administration has to look the other way very often, if not always, and is generally helpless in this matter. The result is, 'we are eating into the capital', as conceded by Shyam Sunder and Yellappa Reddy. They have estimated the annual increment available for removal at about 4.32 million cubic metres in Karnataka; while the government extracts currently 1.7 million cubic metres, the removal on headloads is of the order of 10 million cubic metres.[10] This seems to be a reasonably reliable estimate, since according to an independent estimate by Gadgil and Sinha there is a deficit of 45 lakh tonnes (or 11.25 million cubic metres) in the state after taking into account the fuel needs met by government depots (5 lakh tonnes or 1.25 million cubic metres), dung (5.5 lakh tonnes) and agricultural wastes (52 lakh tonnes).[11] The deficit is obviously met through headloads and/or in a clandestine manner through the over-exploitation of forests.

The extent of deficit met in this way, as estimated by Gadgil and Sinha, varies from region to region within the state. While in the Uttara Kannada zone (excluding the coast) it is 64.4 per cent, which is the highest among the six zones, there is actually a marginal excess or surplus (0.5 per cent) in the northern maidan zone of the state, mainly due to the dominant role played by agricultural wastes in meeting fuel needs. In a region like Uttara Kannada where the area under agriculture

[10] Shyam Sunder and Yellappa Reddy, *op. cit.*, p. 15.

[11] Madhav Gadgil and Madhulika Sinha, The biomass budget of Karnataka, in Saldanha (Ed.), *op. cit.*, p. 24. They assume, however, that the deficit is met from unreserved forests, with the firewood sold through the government coming from reserved forests. Shyam Sunder and Reddy of the Forest Department concede on the other hand that the deficit is met unofficially from reserved forests too.

is quite small (10.6 per cent in 1980–81 which met 28.5 per cent of fuel needs), it is only natural that the major brunt of providing for fuel needs has to be borne by the forests. (Considering the fact that nearly 84 per cent of the area is under forests in the non-coastal part of the district, only 71 per cent of the fuel needs are met, taking into account both the sale from official depots and unofficial exploitation). On the other hand, in the other parts of Western Ghats including Shimoga, the defict met unofficially from forests amounted to only 14.8 per cent while agricultural wastes accounted for 58.7 per cent of the fuel needs, since in this region, a much larger part of the area is cultivated than in Uttara Kannada. In the state as a whole, while 46.2 per cent of fuel needs were met by agricultural wastes (as against 52 per cent of the area under cultivation in 1980–81), the deficit met unofficially from forests was of the order of 20.9 per cent; official depots met only 4.2 per cent of the need[12] (as against 16 per cent of the geographical area under forests in 1980–81).

The official response to such unofficial demand on the forests has been somewhat vacillating—from one of accommodation through releasing more reserved forests (already denuded) and bringing them under the unreserved (protected) category, to one of following the

Table 5.5 Forest Area in Karnataka by Legal Status—1960–61, 1978–79 and 1985–86

(in square kilometres)

Category by Legal Status	*1960–61*	*1978–79*	*1985–86*
Reserved	31715	27947	28611
	(90.2)	(76.9)	(74.0)
Protected	2718	4578	3932
	(7.7)	(12.6)	(10.2)
Village	104	123	124
	(0.3)	(0.3)	(0.3)
Private	—	308	308
		(0.8)	(0.8)
Unclassed	622	3386	5670
	(1.8)	(9.3)	(14.7)
Total	35159	36342	38645

Source: *Annual Administration Report, 1960–61*, Department of Forests, Karnataka, Bangalore; *Karnataka Forest Statistics, 1980*, Department of Forests, Karnataka, Bangalore, 1981; *Annual Report, 1986–87*, Forest Department, Karnataka, Bangalore, 1987.

Note: Figures in brackets are percentages to respective totals.

[12] *Ibid.*, p. 25.

earlier instinct of increasing the extent of reserved forests. The area under reserved forests declined in the state till the late seventies (see Table 5.5), when the first of these reactions can be said to have dominated. Meanwhile, more government lands not earlier under the Forest Department, were placed in charge of this Department resulting in an increase in the 'unclassed forest area', most of which actually did not have much forest cover to speak of. These steps did not help matters to any significant extent. A view was gaining ground in the official circles that an opening of reserve forests to free local privileges led only to denudation, with no one responsible for regeneration. It was thought more desirable in the interest of checking denudation and facilitating regeneration for the Forest Department to allow limited privileges from the reserve forests under proper supervision and control; better still, to make available forest produce directly to the local population free of cost or at nominal prices, without giving access to the forest area directly. Such a view favoured a reversal of the decline under reserve forests, resulting in their increase since the late seventies (see Table 5.5). This was seen in Uttara Kannada as well. The area under reserve forests increased in the district from 7,047 sq. km in 1978–79 to 7,728 sp. kms in 1985–86, the proportion to the total forest area increased in the process from 85 to 93 per cent. Thus, by 1985–86 the Department succeeded in restoring the reserved area in the district close to the early figure of 7,811 sq. kms (as in 1910) at least in size if not in quality. The proportion of reserve forests remained practically the same in Shimoga between 1978–79 and 1985–86 at 59 per cent, with the absolute area declining slightly from 1,962 to 1,946 sq. kms. It should be noted that the situation characterising the old princely State of Mysore, in terms of unreserved forests dominating,[13] no longer prevailed. The districtwise statistics of the Forest Department show that in the districts comprising the old princely State (Mysore, Mandya, Bangalore, Kolar, Tumkur, Hassan, Chikmagalur, Shimoga and Chitradurga), the reserve forests constituted 81 per cent of the total forest area in 1978–79.[14] Though the reserved area remained practically the same in absolute terms, the proportion declined to 70 per cent in 1985–86 mainly due to the addition to the total forest area under the unclassed lands.[15] In spite of this relative decline in recent

[13] See fn 20 in Ch. 3.

[14] Government of Karnataka, Forest Department, *Karnataka Forest Statistics*, Bangalore, 1980, p. 4.

[15] Government of Karnataka, Forest Department, *Annual Report, 1986–87*, p. 42.

years, their dominance is unquestioned in the state including the areas that were under the old princely states.

Having established a virtual monopoly on forest areas, the full responsibility for regeneration of denuded areas and for increasing the production to meet the huge demand on forest produce naturally fell on the Department. Since artificial regeneration is more expensive than natural regeneration, the latter approach has always been preferred by the Department. The Department has been creating conditions favourable for natural regeneration to take place, ever since its establishment, mainly in the form of regulation of commercial exploitation and peoples' access to forests. These forms continued officially in the present phase but in a much more relaxed fashion than in the past, resulting in denudation already referred to. Gap-filling plantations have also been in vogue, whereby gaps are identified in forests and are filled up by planting mixed species. Data on the exact area covered by such regeneration were not available. The Department, however, has statistics on the area covered by artificial regeneration in blocks or clear felled areas. In the state as a whole, 639 thousand hectares were covered thus from 1957–58 to 1983–84, constituting 16.6 per cent of the forest area. The *Annual Administration Report for 1984–85* mentions that in the Kanara Circle, as much as 6,144 sq. kms out of 8,292 sq. kms of forest area (74 per cent) were covered by one system of regeneration or the other.[16] Such a record, however, does not seem to have been achieved in other circles; or such data were not available for other circles. In any case, regeneration efforts have fallen short of requirements, and regeneration does not match with the current rates of exploitation.

Apart from efforts to step up regeneration, an important official reaction to regulate denudation and diversion of rich forest area for developmental projects was in terms of the passing of the Forest Conservation Act of 1980. Section 2 of the Act provides that no state government or other authority shall make, except with the prior approval of the central government, any order directing (a) that any reserved forest . . . . or any portion thereof, shall cease to be reserved; (b) that any forest land or any portion thereof may be used for any non-forest purpose. The Ministry of Environment, Forests and Wildlife at the Centre has to clear the projects of both the state and central

[16] Karnataka Forest Department, *Annual Administration Report for 1984–85*, Bangalore, p. 14.

governments in this regard. It is hoped that this will lead to a healthy restraint on diversion and denudation of forest areas. It is a moot point, however, if the loss of minor and village forests and grazing lands is viewed with an equally serious concern. The general attitude seems to be that these areas are expendable.

Nature and Composition of Demand vis-à-vis Outturn

This policy of bringing more land under the Forest Department particularly under the reserved category is yet to show results in terms of increasing production, though admittedly the extent of denudation is far less in the reserved forests. There has been a downward trend of outturn of major and even minor forest produce to date. Table 5.6 presents official statistics on the outturn of important items of forest produce—both major and minor, which represent only officially permitted extraction. During the mid-eighties, the outturn of both firewood and major forest produce as a whole was almost one-third of the figure during the mid-seventies. The decline in the production of rose and teak wood and timber (sawn, round poles and other kinds together) has been sharper still. The output of charcoal has been highly fluctuating, but in 1984–85 there was a disastrous fall. The decline in bamboo output is by almost one-half. To some extent the outturn declined because the earlier rates of extraction were above sustainable level, while the present rates of extraction (at least official, excluding extraction on headloads) are kept closer to sustainable use by even withdrawing from some of the earlier contracts with some industries. The impact of denudation is also reflected in the declining outturn.

Due to significant shortages, the forest based industries are reported to be importing their requirements from outside the state and even from abroad (as in the case of teak for plywood industry). The requirements of industries (during the early eighties), as seen from the quantities allotted to them, can be seen from Table 5.7. They do not, however, correspond to the consumption of forest produce from Karnataka. A comparison of Tables 5.6 and 5.7 reveals that while the total requirements of industries, excluding bamboo, was 1,744 thousand cubic metres, the outturn of major forest produce including firewood

Table 5.6 Out-turn of Forest Produce in Karnataka, 1976–77 to 1984–85

Products	*1976–77*	*1977–78*	*1978–79*	*1979–80*	*1980–81*	*1981–82*	*1982–83*	*1983–84*	*1984–85*
Major forest produce in '00 $M^3(r)$									
Rose and teak wood	786	961	787	1214	855	595	176	227	161
Timber (including round poles)	6659	6479	5430	3824	3626	2379	2978	2096	1899
Pulpwood	5468	5370	4193	5590	3032	2203	1200	993	1716
Plywood and matchwood	1170	1912	1352	1201	1465	1191	674	528	1006
Firewood	17115	13238	11254	12381	10695	6779	10596	4971	5421
Total—major	31198	27960	23016	24210	19673	13147	15624	8815	10203
Minor forest produce in '00 tonnes									
Bamboo	1689	1437	1452	1002	1436	1707	1278	575	862
Sandalwood (rough)	17	25	18	9	16	8	2	12	20
Charcoal	196	209	41	68	25	0.1	148	2	5
Canes	15	6	6	8	6	11	6	51	28

Source: Government of Karnataka, Forest Department, *Karnataka Forest Statistics 1984*, Bangalore, 1985, p. 16; and Government of Karnataka, Forest Department, *Annual Administration Report for 1984–85*, Bangalore, pp. 16 and 22.

Table 5.7 Requirements of Forest Produce by Industries in Karnataka

Name of Industry	*Forest Produce*	*Unit*	*Quantity Allotted*
Plywood	Softwood	Cubic metres in '00	1071
Matchwood	Softwood	Cubic metres in '00	210
Chipboard	Softwood	Cubic metres in '00	401
Packing cases	Softwood	Cubic metres in '00	71
Paper mills	Bamboo	Tonnes in '00	3090
Paper mills	Eucalyptus	Cubic metres in '00	2760*
Paper mills	Firewood	Cubic metres in '00	1375*
Rayon	Eucalyptus	Cubic metres in '00	5750*
Rayon	Firewood	Cubic metres in '00	500*
Tobacco curing	Firewood	Cubic metres in '00	4500*
Tile manufacturing	Firewood	Cubic metres in '00	800*
Total excluding bamboo		Cubic metres in '00	17438

* Tonnes have been converted to cubic metres here to facilitate comparison with Table 7. (Eucalyptus 1 tonne = 2.3 cu.m; Firewood 1 tonne = 2.5 cu.m).

Source: Government of Karnataka, Department of Forests, *Background paper on forest policy* (prepared for the Economic and Planning Council), November 1983, Mimeo, Annexure X.

distributed for household use amounted to 1,315 thousand cubic metres in 1981–82 and 1,019 thousand cubic metres in 1984–85. It should be noted that the requirements here exclude those of households for firewood, while the outturn includes the same. The gap between requirements and outturn is, therefore, far more than what can be seen from a comparison of Tables 5.6 and 5.7.

It may seem somewhat surprising that even during this phase of dominant industrial use, the major part of the forest produce is allocated to the direct consumption of people, rather than to forest based industries. This is particularly so if the unofficially extracted firewood is taken into account. Even if only the officially extracted forest produce is considered, firewood constituted 55 per cent of the outturn of major forest produce in 1976–77 and 53 per cent in 1984–85. The share of industries vis-à-vis household consumption in firewood use is still not very clear. As per official statistics (Table 5.7), firewood required by industries, as seen from the quantities allotted, amounted to 0.72 million cubic metres during the early eighties, as against the outturn of 1.07 million cubic metres in 1980–81 and 0.5 million cubic metres in 1984–85. However, not all requirements of industries are actually met in practice, and it is not true that practically all the officially extracted firewood is allocated for industrial consumption, as may appear from the figures here. In fact, nearly 5 lakh tonnes or 1.25 million cubic metres of firewood were reported to be distributed through fuel depots,[17] which again implied that practically all the officially extracted firewood (in fact, more than what was extracted) was distributed for household consumption alone. Thus, even if the officially extracted firewood is excluded, the unofficial extraction amounting to over 10 million cubic metres in the state, is far in excess of the total industrial consumption of forest produce being at least five times larger than the latter.

As far as bamboo is concerned, there are no clear data about how much of the officially extracted outturn is used by industries and how much by others (artisans, farmers, etc). Apart from paper mills, bamboo is used by the construction industry for scaffolding and by others for commercial pruposes. But the quantity allotted to paper mills alone far exceeds the outturn, and the actual consumption falls far short of the quantities allotted. However, unlike firewood, commercial consumption including that by industries dominates the use of bamboo.

Summing up about the end use of forest produce, we can say that if firewood is excluded, there is no doubt that practically all the major forest produce and the larger part of the minor forest produce is used commercially by industries. Since firewood, particularly the 'unofficially' extracted type, is used mainly for household consumption, and as this is overwhelmingly more than industrial consumption, household consumption could still be said to dominate in the use of forest produce. This could be true for Uttara Kannada and Shimoga as well.

It is necessary to note here, however, that even non-industrial firewood consumption is not all for local use, nor is it all for subsistence. In fact, most of it is commercialised. A recent study by Bhagavan and Giriappa for Karnataka showed that the bulk of firewood even in rural areas is consumed by the middle class (big and middle farmers and small entrepreneurs), and a large part of it (60 per cent) is purchased. On the other hand, fuel needs of the weaker sections are met mostly by self-produced or self-collected non-firewood biomass, rather than purchases from the market.[18] On the whole, nearly half of the firewood consumption is commercialised in villages, while almost

[17] As per Gadgil and Sinha, *op. cit.*, p. 24.

[18] See M.R. Bhagavan and S. Giriappa, 'Class character of rural energy crisis', *EPW*, Review of Agriculture, 27 June 1987, esp. pp. A–63 and 64.

all the firewood consumption is commercialised in semi-urban and urban areas. The urban consumption of firewood is by no means meagre.[19] The major part of even unofficially extracted firewood is meant for sale and finds it way to semi-urban markets, with only the lops and tops being retained for home use by those who gather wood. Thus we see that consumption by the larger economy still dominates even in regard to firewood, a feature quite consistent with the present stage of forest use. Dominant industrial use of non-firewood forest produce co-exists with the dominant household consumption of firewood, both by the larger economy. In any case, the conceptual purity of an analytical stage need not fully correspond with an empirically identified stage, since the co-existence of different stages of forest use can be quite normal in practice in a country like India which has similar features in other economic sectors too.

Local Reaction

At first the reaction of the local people in Uttara Kannada to the deteriorating supply of fuel, fodder and manure, continued more or less on the same lines as before, namely, asking for more concessions or more areas where privileges could be exercised. Though the privileges continued, extension of areas for exercising them was not granted. Till the eighties, however, forest issues did not figure prominently, as even more important issues engaged the attention of locals. Apart from the freedom movement, agrarian struggles for the regulation of tenancy came to the fore in the forties. The old landlord class in the coastal areas, which was in the forefront of the struggle on forest issues, was in the process of losing its grip on land and with the

[19] Reddy and Reddy who made a study of the energy use in the urban sector, assert, '.... in the urban context, *firewood is non-commercial energy*—it is as commercial a form as electricity, oil or coal'. (Emphasis in original). They have estimated the total consumption of firewood in Karnataka's cities and towns at 2.2 million tonnes (or about 5.5 million cubic metres) a year, which accounts for almost half of the total firewood consumption in the state. Their estimate pertains to household consumption. See A.K.N. Reddy and B. Sudhakar Reddy, 'The energy sector of the metropolis of Bangalore', in Vinod Vyasulu and A.K.N. Reddy (Eds.), *Essays on Bangalore*. Bangalore: KSCST, Indian Institute of Science, 1985, Vol. 3, p. 75.

migration of the majority of them and the transfer of their land to tenants, this class almost disappeared.[20]

The earlier struggles on forest issues were not marked by an environment consciousness, and were aimed merely at gaining more benefits from forest areas. With the rapid depletion of forests, an environment oriented movement was launched to protest against the Forest Department and the industrial use of forests as the factors underlying this depletion. The inspiration came from the Chipko movement in the Himalayas. In Uttara Kannada, this movement took the name of 'Appiko', a Kannada synonym for the Hindi word 'chipko' (to hug a tree to save it). Popular movements to preserve the environment were launched even earlier in the district—against the Bedthi hydroelectric project which would have submerged thousands of hectares of garden land and forests and against marine pollution caused by the caustic soda factory which affected fisheries. The movement against marine pollution was led by the fishermen themselves as their livelihood was being affected.

Thus the conflict of local interests with those of the larger economy emerged on a wider canvas than ever before, and the environmental movement also became more broad-based involving the poorer sections to a greater extent than before. The same people who had sought—in the early days of planned development during the fifties—greater industrialisation and development activities for the region, now began to perceive these activities as anti-local—leading to poverty and misery among the locals rather than to prosperity. The locals began to perceive industrial growth as a case of development of the larger economy at the expense of local interests, promoting underdevelopment of the locals.

Impact of Industrial Use on Local Employment

The disappointment of the locals with development, that is, the market integration of the region with the larger economy, has not been without a basis, apart from the issue of denudation of forests and its

[20] See G.V. Joshi, 'Tenants' movements, land legislation and agrarian change: The case of Uttara Kannada', *Social Science Probings*, Vol. 2 (3), September 1985, pp. 312–52, esp. pp. 350–51.

impact on the locals. It has not even benefited the region in terms of employment generation and earning opportunities outside agriculture, which could have reduced the pressure on land. In spite of the significant industrial use of forest produce, its contribution to employment generation has been marginal, as can be seen from Table 5.8.[21]

The table presents changes in the proportion of workforce to the total population for male and female workers separately, as also in the composition of the workforce from 1901 to 1971 in both Uttara Kannada and Shimoga, and in Karnataka and India as a whole during 1961 and 1971. The detailed classification of workers needed in the preparation of the table was not available for the year 1981. The purpose was not only to assess the role of forest based activities in the composition of the workforce, but also to assess the changes in the level of development of these activities. A forest region in the initial stages may only include primary activities like logging and hunting, but in the more advanced stages it may set up industries for processing forest produce. This development has to be reflected in the changing composition of the workforce. To identify the workforce engaged in forest based activities, the detailed 3-digit industrial classification has to be used. Forests can create indirect employment far beyond the use of their immediate product, but at some stage the contribution of forest produce in the final product of the activity is only an insignificant proportion and cannot be considered a forest based activity. Our listing of workers is based on this consideration.[22] The data collected have been adjusted as far as possible for the changes in definition in terms of the 1916 definition of workforce and regrouped into comparable categories of occupation.[23] It should be noted,

[21] This table as well as the following analysis based on this are taken from Nadkarni and Samuel. 'Population and workforce changes in a forest region', *Social Science Probings*, Vol. I (3), September 1984. See this paper for a fuller discussion of the methodology and census documents used.

[22] The *primary forest sector* consists of hunters and trappers of wild life, wood cutters, charcoal makers and gatherers of minor forest produce. The *seconday* sector consists of basket makers, ivory carvers, cart makers and wheel wrights; makers of mats, screens, thatches, boxes, crates and furniture, workers in processing and manufacturing of wooden, structural and industrial goods like beams, posts, veneer, plywood, tea chests and packing cases; and workers in the pulp, paper and paperboard industry. The *tertiary* sector consists of traders in firewood, timber, bamboos, cane, thatches, furniture, etc., and forest officers and other personnel of the Forest Department. *Cf. ibid*., p. 395.

[23] The procedure has been explained in the Appendix of the paper. *Ibid*., pp. 394–96. The 1961 Census identified a worker as one engaging in some productive or economic work. People like housewives whose main activity is non-economic but secondary activity is economic, were included in the 1961 definition, but not in the 1971 definition.

Table 5.8 Composition of Workforce and Role of Forestry and Forest Based Sectors

Year	TWF* as per cent of Population		Worforce in Agri., Hortic., and Plantations as per cent of TWF		Total Forest Workers as per cent of TWF		Distribution (per cent) of Forest Workers in					
							Primary Forest Sector		Secondary Forest Sector		Tertiary Sector	
	M	F	M	F	M	F	M	F	M	F	M	F
(1)	(2)	(3)	(4)	(5)	(6)	(7)	(8)	(9)	(10)	(11)	(12)	(13)
Uttara Kannada												
1901	66.6	38.7	63.8	69.1	2.0	1.3	2.9	0	69.2	49.9	27.9	50.1
1911	60.7	32.3	66.1	68.8	2.4	1.1	6.3	8.1	61.8	59.3	31.9	32.6
1921	60.6	36.4	65.6	71.3	2.7	1.6	12.3	5.0	56.7	51.9	31.0	43.0
1931	45.0	9.9	63.9	64.1	2.9	2.2	12.6	16.1	76.1	46.5	11.4	37.4
1951	57.0	30.8	64.5	75.6	4.2	1.9	33.3	35.0	50.5	38.1	16.2	26.8
1961	56.8	32.5	58.8	74.2	5.9	2.4	17.3	14.7	68.7	71.1	14.0	14.2
1971	53.1	17.1	59.6	70.1	5.9	4.0	13.4	19.9	67.7	71.8	18.9	8.3

Shimoga												
1901	59.2	23.1	71.2	65.2	1.5	1.7	5.8	0.2	83.2	42.6	11.0	57.2
1911	54.5	15.5	87.6	62.1	1.8	2.4	2.0	2.6	86.4	43.6	11.6	53.7
1921	41.6	10.2	76.2	81.8	2.7	1.6	4.0	0.3	79.8	89.5	16.2	10.2
1931	61.4	30.4	73.2	81.6	2.1	2.3	3.8	0	71.7	45.1	24.5	54.3
1941	55.0	11.9	70.4	72.7	2.3	0.4	2.7	14.4	82.9	80.3	14.4	5.3
1951	50.6	11.0	66.3	71.5	2.9	1.5	18.2	23.9	75.9	74.4	5.9	1.7
1961	58.6	28.3	58.6	74.5	2.7	1.4	11.5	8.3	83.5	87.0	5.0	4.7
1971	51.9	12.2	69.9	82.9	3.0	1.8	8.7	28.5	77.5	59.7	13.8	11.8
Karnataka												
1961	58.4	32.0	68.1	81.3	1.9	1.2	7.7	3.2	80.1	86.2	12.2	10.7
1971	54.6	16.8	66.7	76.6	1.9	1.1	5.2	8.8	78.9	75.0	15.9	16.1
INDIA												
1961	57.1	28.0	65.3	80.4	1.7	1.3	9.3	13.8	76.1	78.2	14.6	8.0
1971	52.6	14.3	67.6	82.3	1.5	1.0	5.6	7.9	75.8	78.7	18.6	13.4

Note: * TWF is Total Workforce; M is male; F is female.
Source: N.V. Nadkarni and M. Johnson Samuel, *op. cit.*, Tables 4, 5 and 5 on pp. 380–85.

however, that even after such adjustments, workers in 1917 are underestimated in terms of the 1961 definition because the secondary economic activity was not recorded in the 1971 Census in all cases. Such underestimation was particularly high in the case of female workers. The data for male or female workers had, therefore, to be presented separately.

As can be seen from the Table 5.8, the bulk of the workforce in the forest region is still concentrated in the agricultural sector (including horticulture and plantation), though in a district like Uttara Kannada the forest area accounted for nearly 80 per cent of the geographical area, and the net cultivated area for only 10 per cent. The proportion of the agricultural workforce is a little less in this district than in the state or in the country as a whole, but this is not the case in Shimoga. Though the absolute size of the workforce engaged in forest based activities (all the three sectors) increased significantly,[24] their proportion in the total workforce increasd from 2 per cent in 1901 to 5.9 per cent in 1971 in Uttara Kannada and from 1.5 per cent to 3 per cent in Shimoga during the same period (in the case of male workers only). The proportion, in contrast, was 1.9 per cent in Karnataka and 1.5 per cent in India in 1971. The difference is not very significant as the proportion remains marginal in the forest region.

As regards the composition of the workforce within forest based activities, there have been quite a few changes in both the districts. The secondary sector has always accounted for the bulk of the male workforce even in the early decades, but the tertiary sector accounted for the bulk of female workers in the early decades. Over the years, the share of the tertiary sector has declined substantially in the female workforce, which was so even in absolute numbers. With the commercialisation of forests, petty traders in forest produce have been displaced and only traders like timber merchants dominate. The sharp decline in the female workforce would suggest that the involvement of women in selling forest produce must have been particularly affected in the process. It is also true, however, that since the extraction of forest produce by female workers is largely a subsidiary activity, it is very likely to be significantly underestimated. On the other hand, there is an improvement in the share of the secondary sector in the female workforce, though not as sharp as to compensate for the decline in the tertiary sector.

[24] The number of male workers increased as between 1901 and 1971 from 3,193 to 13,683 in Uttara Kannada, and 1,071 to 2,854 in Shimoga.

Table 5.9 Subsidiary Employment in Forest Based Activities as against the Main (Both in the Secondary Sector)—Number of Workers

	Uttara Kannada		*Shimoga*	
	Male	*Female*	*Male*	*Female*
1961				
Subsidiary	1726	512	1966	705
Main	8151	1831	7050	1690
1971				
Subsidiary	288	105	352	92
Main	9258	2048	8250	809

Source: Nadkarni and Samuel, *op. cit.*, Table 9, p. 390.

On the whole, the dominance of both the secondary and tertiary sectors from the beginning of the century indicates that a fairly high level of commercialisation had been attained by the turn of the century. However, there have been changes within the secondary and tertiary sectors. Traditional processing activities like basket weaving and cart making were increasingly displaced by the modern sector consisting of paper and board industry and the personnel employed in the Forest Department, particularly in Uttara Kannada. Between 1901 and 1971 the proportion of the modern sector increased from 14 to 46 per cent among males and from 0 to 33 per cent among female workers in Uttara Kannada, while in Shimoga, it increased from 6 to 25 per cent among males and 0.3 to 7 per cent among female workers.[25]

It may be argued that employment in forest based activities is underestimated because the classification of the workforce is on the basis of the main activity, whereas employment in forest based activities can be largely of a subsidiary nature if it is in the household sector. It may be noted here that dependent workers and 'non-workers' with forest occupation (as subsidiary) have already been included in the estimates of the forest workforce. An attempt was made therefore to estimate subsidiary employment in forest related activities in the secondary sector, as against the main activity for 1961 and 1971, and the result of this exercise is presented in Table 5.9. It includes individuals whose main activity is cultivation, agricultural labour, etc., but who are engaged in household industry based on forest produce which is a secondary activity. The table shows that let alone subsidiary employment being more dominant than the main activity, even if it is added to

[25] For details, see Nadkarni and Samuel, *op. cit.*, p. 387.

the main activity, absolute employment in the forest sector is not likely to increase by more than one-fourth.

We can get an idea of how limited employment in forest based activities has been if we relate it to the area under forests. Table 5.10 shows the number of workers in such activities per sq. km. of forest area in 1961 and 1971. Since an estimate of subsidiary employment in

Table 5.10 Number of Workers in Forest Related Activities per square kilometre of Forest Area

	1961			*1971*		
	Male	*Female*	*Total*	*Male*	*Female*	*Total*
Uttara Kannada	1.42	0.31	1.73	1.64	0.34	1.98
Shimoga	5.78	1.33	7.11	5.01	0.64	5.65
Karnataka	4.83	1.64	6.47	5.43	0.88	6.31
India	4.12	1.44	5.56	3.58	0.56	4.14

Source: Nadkarni and Samuel, *op. cit.*, Table 10, p. 391.

forest related activities was available for secondary activities for these years, only main employment has been taken into account. But as we have already seen, the inclusion of subsidiary employment would not have altered the figures radically. The table shows that the employment generated by per sq. km. of forest area is pitifully low, and it even declined in 1971, though Uttara Kannada showed a marginal increase. Even if we ignore the decline, the 1961 levels are quite low, particularly so in Uttara Kannada where the bulk of the area is under forests. We may, however, note that all the employment in forest based activities is direct, and leaves out indirect employment generated by forest produce. It would be difficult to estimate such indirect employment as created by, say, fuel wood and paper. The discussion here is not intended to undermine the importance of forest produce and forest based activities for the rest of the economy.

It is necessary to examine why the increase in employment in modern industry has had only a marginal impact in the region. We have to first determine the extent to which structural features of forest based industries are responsible for this. A few important structural features of these industries taken together, based on the *Annual Survey of Industries* data for three years, 1979–80 to 1981–82 are presented in Table 5.11. The data relate only to the organised factory sector, and exclude unregistered firms.

Table 5.11 A Few Structural Features of Forest Based Industries* in Karnataka vis-à-vis All Industries Together (Average for Three Years: 1979–80 to 1981–82)

(forest based industries are arranged in descending order of capital/output ratios)

Type of Industry	*Industry Code as per ASI*	*Ratio of Fixed Capital to*		*Fixed Capital*		*Ratio of*		*Rate of Profit as per cent Over TC*
		Output	*NAV*	*Per Worker (Rs. in '00)*	*as % of TC*	*NAV to Input*	*TE to NAV*	
(1)	(2)	(3)	(4)	(5)	(6)	(7)	(8)	(9)
1. Pulp and paper including newsprint and paperboard	280	1.73	8.68	1889	90.7	0.28	0.73	0.9
2. Veneer, plywood and products	270	0.27	1.29	138	72.4	0.28	0.69	4.1
3. Wood products, furniture and fixtures other than (2) and (4)	27 excluding 270 and 271	0.22	1.53	56	54.3	0.17	1.97	−41.2
4. Sawing and plaining of wood (other than plywood)	271	0.16	0.56	57	76.8	0.41	0.60	44.2
5. Containers of paper and paperboard	281	0.15	0.88	199	48.8	0.21	0.26	27.3
All industries (including both forest based and all other industries)	—	0.56	2.24	524	71.7	0.36	0.56	7.2

Note: * Includes only the organised factory sector.
NAV is Net Value Added; TC is Total capital, i.e., fixed and working capital;
TE is Total emoluments including supplementary payments like employers' contribution to PF and imputed value of benefits in kind.
Source: Calculated from Government of India, *Annual Survey of Industries*, 1979–80, 1980–81 and 1981–82, Vols. I and II of respective years.

It is obvious from the table that all forest based industries are not alike. The most capital-intensive industry in terms of ratio of fixed capital both to output and to net value added, is the manufacture of paper and pulp. It also requires the highest amount of fixed capital per worker and as a proportion to the total capital. Judged by any of these four criteria, the capital intensity of this industry is more than that of all industries taken together, apart from other forest based industries.

Taking the first three most capital-intensive industries, viz., paper and pulp, veneer and plywood, and other wood products, their profitability is the lowest. Not only do their capital costs run high, even their labour costs are high in terms of total emoluments as a proportion of net value added. On the other hand, other forest based industries—saw-mills (excluding those combining manufacture of plywood and veneer) and container making units—have low capital intensity and high profitability, even higher than that in the organised industrial sector as a whole. Another structural weakness of forest based industries which leads both to low profitability and low employment potential, is the low ratio of net value added to total input. This shows that forest based industries generate a lower level of surplus as shown by the net value added, than the whole organised industrial sector taken together, except for the sawing and plaining of wood (other than plywood and veneer mills) which has a higher ratio of net value added over inputs. This is a reflection of the lower productivity of forest based industries, which is partly because most of them run below capacity due to a shortage of raw material.

We have a clue here as to why the impact of commercial use of forest produce has been marginal in terms of employment generated in the region. The region has mostly weight losing, capital-intensive industries which find it expensive to generate adequate employment. On the other hand, other forest based industries are spread out, and the forest region does not benefit much from them. However, there are constraints on multiplying these labour-intensive industries due to the inadequate availability of forest produce. As such, the employment potential generated by the forest based sector has been marginal for both these reasons.

Thus we see that the dominant industries phase has run into serious constraints in its development. The forest based industries do not function on healthy lines, apart from the problems of low productivity in the primary forest sector. In fact, even the contribution of forestry and logging to the State Domestic Product (SDP) in constant prices has been steadily decreasing, even while the unsustainable use of forests is continuing. The SDP originating from forestry and logging at constant prices stood at Rs. 40.78 crores in 1970–71 and Rs. 31.16 crores in 1980–81.[26]

[26] Based on SDP data obtained from the Directorate of Economics and Statistics, Karnataka. It may also be noted that as a proportion of the total net State Domestic Product, the contribution from forestry and logging stood at 2.1 per cent in Karnataka in 1970–71, at 1.4 per cent in 1980–81 at 1970–71 prices and at 1.9 per cent at current prices. In the country as a whole, the same as a per cent of the total net domestic product from all sectors stood at only 1.2 per cent in 1970–71, and at 0.7 per cent in 1980–81 and 0.9 per cent in 1985–86 at current prices. Though the prices (implicit) of forestry and logging rose much faster than those of all commodities, this did not help in preventing a decline in the contribution of this sector (in per cent) at current prices. (The national figures are calculated on the basis of statistics in Government of India, Directorate of Economics and Statistics, *Indian agriculture in brief*, 1987, 21st edition, pp. 5, 6).

Chapter Six

Towards an Enlightened Stage?

Populist Positions, Bureaucratic Solutions

More than a century has passed since the establishment of the Forest Department and the introduction of scientific forestry with the explicit purpose of fulfilling the role of conserving forests. This Department had to shoulder the difficult responsibility of regulating both the commercial and local exploitation in the interest of sustainable use. The state was expected not only to be the most powerful among the three parties involved, but also the most committed to the cause of conservation. Today, we do not seem to be any closer to the enlightened stage than we were a century ago, inspite of the vast official machinery built up by the Department. The most critical test was during the Second World War and the subsequent period of the dominant industrial phase that began with it. The Department was literally swept off its feet by the unprecedented demand from the industries as well as from the population both in the larger and the local economy.[1] The conservation bias of the Department could not stand on its own against

[1] Romm has aptly observed,

> Historically, the fate of forests has been determined by forces other than conscious decisions about how forests are or should be used. Population growth has reduced the forest when available technologies or markets did not support adequate intensification of agriculture and other economic activities to absorb people without clearing new lands. The forests have fragmented when social pressures to evade or modify governmental authority exceeded governmental powers to control them; they have remained in tact when governmental powers over forest lands were unambiguous.

Cf. Jeff Romm, 'Forest policy and development policy', *Journal of World Forest Resource Management*, Vol. 2, 1986, p. 85.

the strong forces of the larger economy. After all, the state is a political organ and in the political struggle for domination over forests, the cause of conservation had little support.

The current situation constitutes a serious crisis. The gap between the demand for and the availability of forest produce is wide and is continuously increasing. As a result forests are vanishing at a rapid pace of nearly 1.5 million hectares per year, as assessed from the satellite imagery. This has led to a sharp indictment of the Forest Department since the crisis has been attributed to the alienation of the locals from the forests caused by the Department as well as to the almost unsatiable demand for cheap forest resources from the larger economy which the Department failed to check. In other words, the subjugation of locals in the political struggle for natural resources is considered to be the major factor leading to this. The truth, however, seems to be far more complex than is assumed by this criticism.

First, the assumption that locals are the most committed to the cause of conservation, as well as the most competent to take care of it, is itself questionable, even after conceding that several local communities have shown remarkable evidence of both commitment to conservation and traditional knowledge about the same. We will explore the nature and extent of forest exploitation by the locals, and identify constraints in the locals' ability for and commitment to conservation later. There are not only serious constraints to this, but also the dichotomy between the local *versus* the larger economy in terms of subsistence and profit motivation is itself neither sharp nor meaningful. The most poignant part of the local use of forests is that while forest produce is obtained free, the garden economy for which it is used is highly commercial and profit motivated and not just for the subsistence of the poor. The class differentiation within the local economy is hardly insignificant, and constrains the local commitment to conservation.

Second, it is incorrect to take for granted that locals have been alienated from the use of forests. We have to distinguish between alienation in terms of use and alienation in terms of management of forests. The basic feature of forest organisation has been government ownership and management, achieved through a long and painful process in the face of stiff resistance from the local population. This has alienated the local population from the management of forests in the case of reserve forests, but not in the case of minor forests and village forests. But even in the case of reserve forests, the locals could not be excluded from their use. Though in the struggle for the use of forests between the locals and the larger economy, the latter has always been dominant, yet it could not exclude the locals. There had to be accommodation and compromise with the locals, achieved through decades of struggle and adjustment. Not only was free access permitted in the non-reserved forests, privileges were granted even in reserve forests. Unfortunately, no local institutions were developed to take care of such forests where free access was permitted to ensure their sustainable use. As a result, the degradation of areas that were left free for local use was complete. Politicians yielded to local pressures and handed over forests and grazing lands under common property for private cultivation. Market forces also aided this process.[2] Whatever forests exist today are in reserved areas, in spite of the exploitation by commercial interests. We can well imagine what the consequence would have been if any populist view that forests should be de-reserved and passed on to local peoples' control is taken seriously, particularly when no dependable machinery is on the horizon which can take care of village and community forests, let alone all forest areas including the reserved.

It is necessary to appreciate that forces of commercialisation are not unique to the larger economy, and have affected the locals in their attitude, even if their use of forests continues outside the market framework. The rise of cash economy in most rural transactions and the gradual replacement of subsistence agriculture by commercial agriculture have changed rural attitudes towards resource use and their management, making them more individualistic and less communitarian. Maximisation decisions take place at the household level, and rarely at the community level.[3] Such a trend was certainly not favourable for conservation, since it needed a communitarian ethos. Thus, even if local communities had made a sustainable use of forests in the pre-commercial past, it cannot be assumed that they can do so today without any monitoring and regulatory power exercised by the state to ensure their proper use.

Third, it is incorrect to assume that even during the stage of dominance of industry, the industrial use of forests is the major source of pressure on them. It was observed earlier that the demand for fuel

[2] See N.S. Jodha, 'Market forces and erosion of common property resources', in ICRISAT, *Agricultural markets in semi-arid tropics*. Patancheru, Andhra Pradesh, 1985.

[3] See M.V. Nadkarni, 'Agricultural development and ecology—An economist's view', *Indian Journal of Agricultural Economics*, Vol. 42(3), July–September 1987, esp. pp. 370–71.

wood for household consumption was about five times higher than the total demand from industries in Karnataka, though the bulk of fuel wood consumption is already commercialised and is not restricted to the local economy of the forest region. But even within the forest region, local pressure on forests shows no sign of abatement. Forest industries did not create sufficient employment opportunities for the locals to reduce their dependence on land. In agriculture, the holdings are small in the forest region, and they cannot be a significant source of either fuel or fodder. The economy of even rich cultivators is dependent on the forests for viability of both cultivation and livestock. The demand for more land continues unabated, chiefly at the expense of forests, both for cultivation and for fuel and fodder.

This discussion does not imply that all was well with forest management, and only the locals were to blame. British contempt for locals and their assumption that scientific forestry precluded the involvement of locals in management was built into the very conception and establishment of the whole organisation of the Forest Department. This led to purely bureaucratic and professional or technocratic solutions. In other words, forestry or forest management was viewed only as a technical problem, without trying to assess the implications of technical solutions for the locals and the impact they would have on the local economy. This only served to sharpen the divide between the Department and the locals population, and more and more emphasis was laid on policing the forests. The Department became a symbol of oppression to the locals.[4]

Even in terms of developing a professional or a scientific basis for forestry, the practice of forestry did not seem to have been ideal. The emphasis was more on administration and policing than on developing scientific forestry at all levels, though the Department lacked neither expertise nor research of a high calibre and perspective. Gadgil *et al.* have pointed out that the Department did not have accurate information about basic facts like land under its control, the extent of standing crop and productivity of forests under its control, and the extent of removal of fuel wood. They have further observed on the basis of research work by eminent foresters that the Department did not have

[4] The 'professional' view focuses on 'the dynamics of the forest rather than upon the social and governmental behaviour that determines them . . . . Where professionals have governed forest policy making, policies are often normative statements of purpose that seem inevitably thwarted by society's possibly malicious refusal to stand still'. *Cf.* Romm, *op. cit.*, p. 86.

a scientific and dependable criteria about how many trees could be cut per hectare and with what time interval for ensuring sustainable use.[5] The statistical base needed for scientific forestry remains inadequate to date. For example, the Department still does not have estimates of demand for and supply of forest produce, as against the estimate of desirable extraction permitted by sustainable use either for different types of major forest produce or at the aggregate level.

Unfortunately, the Department did not even develop a proper perception of the scarcity of forest produce, partly because of the inadequate economic and statistical information required, and largely because of lack of interest thanks to the pressures of the larger economy. This resulted in an extremely unscientific and ecologically ruinous pricing of forest produce given over to industry. Strictly speaking, till recently forest produce was not priced at all, as only royalty was paid to the Department for extraction. In a sense this was uncharacteristic of a monopoly supplier, who is supposed to be restricting supply and keeping the price high in order to maximise profits. Let alone the price being more than the cost of production (regeneration), it did not even cover it. There was no question of covering the cost of extraction, as it was carried out by private contractors. What the Department received was a nominal rent which was enough to cover the cost of establishment and leave some surplus.

In discussing the various stages of forest use and management earlier, it was observed that only during the pre-commercial stage forest produce was considered to be abundant and that the perception of scarcity of forest produce began to develop only with the commercialisation of forests. Since, however, commercialisation advanced perched firmly on the shoulders of colonialism and the market for forest produce was hardly competitive, the environment was not conducive to develop a proper perception of scarcity. Even otherwise, the scarcity of *in situ* natural resources is hardly perceived in general by the market, where prices are based on the cost of extraction.

This was dominant in the case of forest produce, except to some extent in a few items like ivory, sandalwood and teak. The cost of regeneration was hardly the main criterion in the pricing of forest produce. This was directly responsible for its wanton extraction and deforestation. An enlightened stage of forest use can be based only on a proper perception of the *in situ* scarcity of forest produce.

[5] *Cf.* Madhav Gadgil, S.N. Prasad and Rauf Ali, *Forest management in India: A critical review*, Centre for Theoretical Studies, Indian Institute of Science, Bangalore, 1982, Mimeo, pp. 25–26.

Towards Corrective Steps

We may recall that an enlightened stage of forest use and management can be said to be reached, when exploitation is on a sustainable basis, providing for regeneration and satisfaction of both the locals and the larger economy in a harmonious way. Clearly, it calls for radical corrective steps on all fronts—technical, economic and institutional. The physical possibilities of reaching this stage in India are not remote, but within reach. Even if we earmark ecologically sensitive areas to be completely free from exploitation, we still have vast areas which are already deforested and other wastelands. A reforestation of these areas would not only provide immediate employment but could contribute towards bridging the gap between demand and supply of forest produce including fuel wood.

Table 6.1 Wasteland Availability in Karnataka

Districts	*Vacant Government Wasteland Available in '000 Hectares*	*As per cent of Geographical Area*	*Transferred to Forest Department (Categorised as 'C' and 'D' Class Lands) in '000 Hectares*
(1)	*(2)*	*(3)*	*(4)*
Uttara Kannada	14	1.3	Nil
Shimoga	477	45.1	72
Karnataka	3623	19.0	505

Source: Government of Karnataka, Forest Department, *Karnataka Forest Statistics, 1984*, Bangalore, 1985; based on Tables 1 and 13, pp. 5 and 25.

The official sources have identified government owned vacant land that is neither under trees nor under the plough, a part of which has already been surveyed, categorised (as 'C' and 'D' class lands) and transferred to the Forest Department (see Table 6.1). These wastelands, including those not yet transferred, constituted about 19 per cent of the land in the state, and as much as 45 per cent in Shimoga.[6] This estimate may be a little exaggerated, but even if half of it could be afforested to meet peoples' needs of fuel and fodder, shortages in this regard could be overcome.

[6] In the country as a whole, 32.8 million hectares or 10 per cent of the geographical area is estimated to be cultivable waste based on satellite imagery. *Cf.* S. Muthiah (Ed.), *A social and economic atlas of India*. Delhi: Oxford University Press, 1987, p. 98.

Even the area already under forests is not productive enough. It has been acknowledged by an eminent forester that considering the area under evergreen forests in Karnataka (estimate at 4.35 lakh hectares)

> *situated in the most luxuriant climate, the forests should easily put on an increment of 5 m^3 per hectare per annum. If a modest estimate of 3 m^3 of merchantable increment per hectare per annum is reckoned, the annual increment of exploitable timber comes to 13,05,000 m^3, say 1.3 million m^3. Have a look at the annual yield taken out of evergreen forests. It is a dismal 0.25 million m^3 even after accounting for branchwood removed.*[7]

The low rate of incremental yields in forests is generally attributed by the Forest Department officials to the local use of forests even in reserved areas, not only through grazing and heavy pruning of trees (even if the main stand is not cut) for firewood, but also through such destructive practices as causing a fire in the forest area to ensure generation of grass. The reserved forests were never really totally enclosed to prevent local access.[8] Besides, all forest areas cannot be used for production forestry. Under conservation oriented forestry, annual increments could be lower, but this is compensated by the avoidance of environmental costs associated with production forestry involving plantation on clear felled areas.

The problem of what could be the best institutional arrangement for the management of forests particularly for bringing wastelands and deforested areas under forests is difficult. The solution is still at an experimental stage, and cannot be uniform for all types of forests and areas. The Forest Department was not unaware of its bureaucratic nature and had from time to time sought ways of securing peoples' participation in forest development. The experiment with advisory committees in Uttara Kannada (from 1928 to 1942) has already been referred to. However, they could not have succeeded by themselves in overcoming the alienation of locals from forest management and regeneration though they succeeded in extracting more concessions for the locals in forest use by voicing local grievances. There was neither any machinery nor any direct personal incentives to motivate

[7] N.S. Adkoli, 'Trees for survival', National Seminar on Forests and Environment, Department of Forests, Karnataka, Bangalore, 1981.

[8] This author was taken by the foresters to a few reserved forests in the Sirisi division of Uttara Kannada where local use was significant, and to forests where it was not significant due to their being in the interior or farther from human settlements. The latter had much more luxuriant growth.

people to grow trees. Growing trees in community forest areas like minor forests was nobody's business. Forest areas under private control like bettas degraded more slowly, but even in this case regeneration through deliberate plantation was marginal.

However, as early as in 1941, S.S. Dhareshwar, then a junior forest officer in Uttara Kannada, presented certain proposals of far-reaching significance. Noting that minor forests had reached extremely low levels of productivity, which adversely affected their potential of being useful to locals in exercising their privileges, he proposed that they could be leased out in viable holdings—by attaching some areas from reserved forests if necessary—to farmers for regeneration and improving their productivity. Preferably, they were to be entrusted to co-operative farming societies. Plantation could take place under the supervision of the Forest Department, and the holdings could be leased out for a period of eight to ten years at a stretch. Before the plants grew, farmers could be allowed to cultivate millets like ragi and other crops, and of course grass, in the land available, without having to pay land revenue. His proposal involved a close integration of agriculture with forestry and sought to end the alienation of farmers from forests and their regeneration.[9] Such ideas, however, did not find favour with the government till the eighties, mainly because any transfer of forest land to private control was used almost wholly for cultivation of annual agricultural crops, and the government did not have the necessary machinery to monitor and ensure that such lands would be used for regeneration of forests.

These ideas have been revived again. Degraded lands, designated under 'C' and 'D' classes, unfit for economic cultivation but amenable for afforestation, are now under the Forest Department, and more such lands are being transferred to the Department. All these lands are not proposed to be worked directly by the Department itself. Instead of relying on only one type of institutional agency, the emphasis is now on trying out different alternatives—corporations floated by the Department to take care of plantations to meet the needs of pulpwood required by industries, co-operative societies, individual farmers, as well as village based local government bodies like the Mandal Panchayats.

Some of the forest areas and wastelands are already under the

[9] As reported in *KV*, 13 January 1941. Also see S.S. Dhareshwar, 'The denuded condition of the minor forest in Kanara coastal tract, its history and a scheme for its regeneration', *Indian Forester*, Vol. 68, 1941, pp. 68–81.

ka Forest Plantations Corporation (KFPC) and some are given on a long lease to joint sector companies (owned by KFPC and private companies using forest produce) to raise plantations. One-eighth of the eucalyptus produce of KFPC is to be supplied to the Forest Department for onward supply to the rural people, and the rest to private companies at prevailing market prices. About 5 per cent of the species to be planted in such lands are expected to yield fodder and fuel, and villagers would be allowed to take headloads of branches and leaves free of cost. However, no new plantation for raising raw material for industries on forest lands is permitted either directly or under joint sector projects, following a policy decision by the Ministry of Environment and Forests, Government of India, in August 1987. This indicates that forest lands are expected mainly to meet the need for conservation and people's needs for fodder and fuel, and not as a source of raw material even if on the basis of ensuring regeneration. It is feared that such commercial plantations could lead to clear felling of natural forests and would be at the cost of both conservation and people's needs. As far as meeting the needs of industries for raw material is concerned, the policy was to 'enable the small and marginal farmers to produce raw materials for industries on degraded lands available with them'.[10] Since a large proportion of land, particularly uncultivated and less fertile, lies in bigger holdings, it is obvious that small and marginal farmers can hardly meet these needs. Individual farmers, particularly large farmers, have been raising eucalyptus and casurina plantations on relatively infertile parts of their holdings in semi-arid or drought prone regions of Karnataka, though not in Uttara Kannada. The yield of annual agricultural crops on such lands is considered both low and uncertain. Of late, even small farmers have joined in this as it frees them for employment in more lucrative jobs outside agriculture.[11]

A new scheme has been floated to involve landless labour, parti-

[10] *Cf.* 'Government policy on use of forest land for raising plantations for raw material for industries by private firms or individuals', *Wastelands News*, Vol. 3(2), November 1987–January 1988, p. 9.

[11] In the course of a recent study of Kolar district in Karnataka, it was found that 'the cultivation of eucalyptus is mainly taken up by medium and large farmers . . . . small and marginal farmers tend to take to eucalyptus cultivation only when the returns from the existing crops are very low and there exists some alternative employment opportunity.' *Cf.* R.S. Deshpande and H. Chandrashekar, 'Is eucalyptus farming really uneconomic?', in *Workshop on Eucalyptus Plantation*, Bangalore, Indian Statistical Institute, 1984, esp. pp. 175–76.

cularly scheduled castes and tribes, in raising trees on 'C' and 'D' class lands leased to them, either as individuals or as co-operative associations, and also to local institutions like panchayats. Known as the *Tree Patta Scheme*, it gives legal status in respect of usufructuary rights in trees but not land. The beneficiaries have to raise trees within two years of lease and take care of them. Different states including Karnataka, have drawn up their own schemes in this regard. The Karnataka scheme proposes a subsidy on the establishment and maintenance costs of marginal and small farmers. The lessees cannot use the land for agriculture or plantation crops like rubber, coconut or coffee, but only for fuel, fodder or fruit bearing trees. Only if the government resumes the land for any public purpose, the lessee shall have the right to cut the trees for wood.[12]

Social forestry schemes involving roadside planting, community or village lands, green belts around cities are also in progress to meet fodder and fuel needs, with an active involvement of local government agencies.

The garden owners with *betta* lands under their control are being encouraged to grow trees and regenerate them, on the understanding that they can keep at least 25 per cent of the timber grown by them. Perhaps the first attempt at the restoration of bettas with the active involvement of gardeners was initiated by the Hulgol Group Villages Co-operative Service Society at Bhairumbe in Sirsi taluk. The organisation has sought to increase fodder resources in general and modernise animal husbandry practices including discouragement of free grazing. 'A major limitation of this effort was the restriction of involvement to better off farmers of a literate higher caste, the Haviks. This is now sought to be overcome through the establishment of a broader based voluntary agency dedicated to eco-developmental efforts, the Sahyadri Parisara Vardhini'.[13]

Ultimately, the success of an institutional agency is determined by the incentive it has in growing trees and the share of benefits of growing trees enjoyed by it. Such an incentive is admittedly ensured in the case of Forest Plantation Corporations, whether state-owned or joint, and also in the case of individual farmers growing trees on their

[12] For details, see, 'Tree patta scheme', *Wastelands News*, Vol. 2(1), August–October 1986, p. 12; Vol. 2(4), May–July 1987, pp. 26–27.

[13] *Cf.* Madhav Gadgil, K.M. Hegde and K.A. Bhoja Shetty, 'Uttara Kannada—A case study in hill area development', in Cecil J. Saldanha *et al., Karnataka—State of environment report 1985–86*. Bangalore, 1987, p. 161.

holdings (owned or leased in). It may appear therefore, that these are the best suited agencies. Between the two, since the costs are lower in their case, it is easy to pronounce that private farmers are the most suited particularly if they are offered attractive prices for wood. The matter, however, is not as simple as it appears. First, on lands owned by the Forest Department but under private control (like bettas) or on lease, the incentives to 'tenants' are not yet considered attractive enough. They demand full share with nominal cash rent, or at least two-thirds share with no cash rent. Apart from *bettas* which have already been under private control, not much government land has been given out on private lease as forest holdings as yet. The administrative machinery to ensure that they remain forest holdings under good and productive management, and to prevent transfer to large farmers, is yet to evolve.

Second, private agencies cater mainly to the needs of industries using softwood. Though it is not uncommon to find farmers selling their wood (especially casurina) to fuel and timber depots, even here they cater to commercial needs. These agencies could ease the pressure on natural forests in so far as commercial needs are satisfied by them. But they are not in a position to meet non-commercial needs of village communities both for fuel and fodder. Even when Mandal Panchayats are assured of incentives by enabling them to have a due share in the wood grown by them on community lands, there is a risk that they may sell their share to commercial interests to improve their finances. Since local governments are perpetually short of funds, this can be seen as an attractive commercial proposition, rather than as a proposition to meet people's needs. In a commercialised setting, it is indeed hard to find an agency to meet people's needs for fuel and fodder at a non-commercial level.

In the face of such difficulties, the Forest Department itself has taken the responsibility for increasing the availability of firewood and timber for rural people at concessional rates, or even free. The reservation of one-eighth of the produce of the KFPC has already been discussed. The eucalyptus produced in the Department plantations in areas receiving less than 25" of rainfall (including those raised under various schemes like NREP and DPAP) are now reserved entirely for the rural people, and concessions and access which paper and pulp industries had once enjoyed in these areas have now been withdrawn.[14]

[14] *Cf.* Circular letter from the Office of the Conservator of Forests, Bangalore, dated 4-8-1985, No. A6.I.ND.44/82–83.

Ultimately, if other institutional agencies fail to produce enough firewood for supply at concessional rates to the public, the Forest Department would be compelled to undertake this task in the wastelands available. This task could be assigned to a Firewood Plantation Corporation, which could undertake this job as a commercially viable project, with finances provided by banks, instead of depending on the budgetary resources of the government. This need not preclude the Corporation from reserving a part of the produce to meet the needs of the rural poor on a concessional or free basis.[15]

The Department has also undertaken plantations in degraded village forests by enclosing parts of them on the understanding that after they have grown to non-browsable heights, grazing could be allowed, and that firewood would be supplied on a sustainable basis at free or concessional rates. These schemes have not always had a smooth sailing where alternative grazing areas were not available. The Department is aware that unless steps are taken to grow the firewood needed by people, the forests will vanish irrespective of reservation.[16]

Though the institutional problem is yet to be properly resolved, particularly in the case of social forestry projects, there have been two developments favourable to sustainable forestry. The more significant of the two was the decision to abolish the old system of royalty rates, under which forest produce was supplied to industries at lower than market prices and replacement costs. Through an amendment of the Forest Act, the earlier agreements with industries on pricing were annulled. With this change, the policy has been to fix prices on the basis of replacement cost plus 20 per cent margin. The new prices, known as seigniorage rates, came into effect from June 1982, and were again revised with effect from April 1985. As a result of the strong representations from the plywood, matchwood and packing case industries, the rates were moderated in April 1986. A special concession was granted to the government owned Mysore Paper Mills, by charging only 50 per cent of the seigniorage rates for bamboo and eucalyptus supplied for the production of newsprint only, but not for

[15] See M.V. Nadkarni and G.V.K. Rao, 'Fuel wood requirements-I—role of public sector, II—need for timely action', *Economic Times*, 24 and 25 June 1987. It has been argued in this article that the KFPC should reorient its priority to meeting fuel wood needs.

[16] This, according to the Department, was why priority was given to quick growing trees like casurina, acacia auriculiformis, eucalyptus and prosopis juliflora. See Shyam Sunder and Yellappa Reddy, *op. cit.*, p. 17.

other products.[17] In spite of the moderation, the new rates are substantially higher than in the past. The present policy is to revise prices every two years in the light of trends in replacement costs, instead of being tied down by long-term agreements as in the past. The earlier system had been in favour of industries and had discriminated against rural artisans and other rural people. The new policy has now reversed this discrimination, rural people are charged significantly lower rates. For example, the rate for bamboo charged to basket weavers is about 40 per cent less than what is charged to industry, calculated on per tonne basis. The pricing system is on a much more rational and socially defensible basis than ever before.

The second development relates to the abolition of the private contractor system in 1979, which plugged an organisational loophole in the interest of sustainable forestry. This system applied to activities where the Forest Department used to engage contractors for the extraction of forest produce. Even after this abolition, private extraction has continued in forest areas leased out to industries for exclusive allotment where the companies may employ private contractors. This type of extraction is also subject to the new system of rates. The policy is that ultimately the government should take over all extraction, either through the KFPC or the Department directly, though in a phased manner, allowing the current lease agreements to come to an end.

In addition to these steps on the organisational front and on the price front, the Forest Department has also been trying to reduce the pressure on forests through encouraging desirable technological changes. Fuel efficient *chulas* or hearths are being promoted to cut down wasteful use of fuel wood, particularly in the forest region. Even solar cookers are being promoted, though they have not become popular as they are expensive and have to be kept outdoors. These efforts seem to be focused more on the households than industries. Small industries and brick kilns using firewood are yet to witness major improvements in fuel use efficiency. Even at the household level, the adoption rate has not been very high as seen from our study of selected villages in the region.

Can we say that the corrective steps discussed here would reverse the degradation of forests and that forest use and management could be said to be heading towards an enlightened stage conceptualised by us? It is empirically early to expect any tangible results, but there is

[17] See *Annual Report of the Karnataka Forest Department for 1986–87*, pp. 8–9.

some ground for optimism that prospects for such a reversal are not bleak. This is primarily because there is a realisation even in official circles that the traditional approach was unsatisfactory which was based on policing and concentrating only on maintaining the productivity of reserved forests, without bothering to step up the supplies of fuel and fodder for people. The 'professional' approach has been increasingly adapting itself to the socio-economic environment. That is, forestry is no longer seen in isolation as a technical problem. This is a positive development and has motivated the Department to share the fruits of its regeneration efforts with the locals. The irrational enthusiasm for encouraging indiscriminate industrial use at throw-away prices has also been overcome by necessity. At the same time, the other extreme of a populist solution of giving a free access to people to all forests has been avoided. A false perception of the forest produce being free and abundant is inherent in an unconditional and free access, and there would be no interest in regeneration. The attempt has been to strike a balance between 'policing' and 'free access' approaches, so that the perception of scarcity is not lost and incentive for regeneration is maintained. This is by no means an easy task and would require institutional innovations to involve people both in meeting their needs and in regeneration. The necessity for such innovations and efforts is all the more urgent, because there are no bright prospects of a significant diversification of the regional economy and reduced dependence on agriculture or land which could have reduced local pressures on forests.

Part II

The Class Character of the Local Economy and its Forest Dependence

Chapter Seven

Land Use and Abuse

Class Structure in Local Villages

The study of the local economy in a forest region is basically to understand the nature and magnitude of local pressure on forests. This study examines the way in which land is used, the magnitude of encroachment upon forest lands, and the dependence of the local economy on the direct use of forests. These issues have essentially a class dimension; hence the study will show which classes of rural society benefit more from a free access to forests—forest land as well as forest produce. This study of intra-local political economy is intended not only to complement the political economy of the relation between the local vis-à-vis the larger economy, it also throws light on the constraints on environmental care by the locals in a stratified and commercialised setting.

The focus of this study of local economy is on four small villages in the Sirsi forest division of Uttara Kannada district, two of them in Sirsi taluk—Gadihalli and Somanalli, and two in Siddapur taluk—Kangod Kansur and Haldot. The Sirsi division area is very much in the forest region of the district and was in the forefront of the struggles against the Forest Department during the British régime. The reason for selecting four villages instead of only one or two, was to capture variations, if any, in class structure as well as in the nature and extent of forest dependence. The selected villages were smaller than the average and were closer to forests than other villages. Most of the villages close to forests are small, the bigger ones are more urbanised. In all, ninety-two households were covered on census basis—twenty-seven in Gadihalli, twenty-two in Somanalli, thirty-two in Kangod Kansur and eleven in Haldot. The total number of households in each village was verified from village records, and all households in these four villages were covered. No claim is made here that the selected villages can account for all villages in the district, but they are certainly typical of villages close to forests.

Another village, Bharatipur, in the Tirthahalli taluka of Shimoga district was also studied for the limited purpose of comparing the arecanut economy as between two situations—one with the betta privileges as in Uttara Kannada, and the other without these privileges as in Bharatipur. Only twenty garden cultivating households were covered in this village and other types of households were excluded. This village is also in a forest region, but the forests are more degraded and, consequently, the dependence of agriculture on forests is less than in Sirsi division. We may recall here that the proportion of forests is far less in Shimoga district, and the extent of both cultivated lands and wastelands is far more. Being confined to a smaller area, the cultivators' pressure on forests is naturally far greater in Uttara Kannada. The total number of households studied in all the five villages was 112. However, our analysis relates mainly to ninety-two households in Uttara Kannada. The fieldwork for this study was done in the middle of 1986, and the data relate to 1985–86. Several prior trips were made to the region before the canvassing of schedules, covering surrounding villages and forests as well.

Table 7.1 Class-wise Distribution of Households

Class of Households		*Gadihalli*	*Somanalli*	*Kangod Kansur*	*Haldot*	*All Four*
Landlords	a	3	7	2	2	14
	b	11.1	31.8	6.3	18.2	15.2
Capitalist	a	7	3	1	3	14
farmers	b	25.9	13.6	3.1	27.2	15.2
Middle	a	2	—	2	—	4
peasants	b	7.4		6.3		4.3
Poor	a	6	4	11	4	25
peasants	b	22.2	18.2	34.3	36.4	27.2
Agricultural	a	9	6	14	2	31
labour	b	33.3	27.3	43.7	18.2	33.7
Service	a	—	2	2	—	4
class	b		9.1	6.3		4.3
Total	a	27	22	32	11	92
	b	100	100	100	100	100

Note: The percentages here (b) can be compared with class-wise share in different types of land given in Table 7.5.

a is number of households; b is per cent share of the class in the total number.

One of the ways of understanding the class hierarchy in this region is to divide households into garden or plantation owners, paddy cultivators and landless labourers in descending order. In practice, however, a significant number of gardeners cultivate paddy lands as well, mainly through hired labour. On the other hand, quite a few labourers own and operate tiny holdings of paddy land. A more satisfactory framework appeared to be one based on a comparison of own or family labour with the magnitude of hired labour. Accordingly, six classes were identified in the rural society (see Table 7.1).

1. Landlords operate land only on the basis of hired-in labour, their own or family labour is of a supervisory nature; that is, own manual labour is insignificant or zero. There were fourteen landlords out of ninety-two covered in the four villages (15 per cent), all of whom were gardeners.
2. Capitalist farmers contribute their own manual labour, but their agricultural operations are mainly carried out on the basis of hired-in labour. That is, hired-in labour significantly exceeds own and family labour. There were fourteen households in this category (15 per cent), thirteen were gardeners and one cultivated paddy land alone. In terms of social structure, both these classes could be combined.
3. Middle peasants: In their case, own or family labour is more or less equal to hired-in labour, the difference being in the range of ±10 per cent. There were only four households in this category (4 per cent), all of them being gardeners. This class appeared to be closer to capitalist farmers in terms of socio-economic status than to poor peasants.
4. Poor peasants operate their land mainly on the basis of their own/family labour, and either do not need or cannot afford hired-in labour. That is, hired-in labour, if at all, is significantly less than family labour, unlike the other three classes. However, hiring out of labour is not used as a criterion here for the identification of this and the three higher classes. As a matter of fact, hiring out labour was occasional, if at all, among the bulk of poor peasants, and not a major source of income. Thus, they stood distinctly apart and above as compared to agricultural labourers. There were twenty-five households in this category (27 per cent of the total), seven cultivating gardens and eighteen cultivating paddy lands alone.
5. Landless labourers do not own or operate any holdings and earn

their living mainly through hiring out labour either on a casual or attached basis. There were thirty-one such households out of ninety-two covered (34 per cent).

6. Service class consists of teachers, forest guards, etc., i.e., those whose main source of income is service on salaried basis, either in government departments or private undertakings. They are mostly immigrants. They are actually not an organic part of the rural structure of the villages concerned. There were however only four such households (4 per cent) in all the four villages together; two each in Somanalli and Kangod Kansur. The attached or permanent agricutural labour households are not included here.

It may be noted that there were no households belonging to scheduled tribes in any of the villages studied. There were only two scheduled caste households, both engaged in paddy cultivation. The dominant community was the Havyaka brahmins, accounting for thirty-five out of ninety-two households. They were also the richest. All the fourteen landlords and thirteen capitalist farmers, and thirty-three gardeners belonged to this community. Other communities comprised the Naiks, goldsmiths and artisan castes. Surprisingly, there was one Havyaka household in the class of agricultural labourers; there were eighteen households from intermediate castes like Naiks and Kari Vokkaligas in this class.

While the upper caste households had more or less concentrated on agriculture including gardening, the economy of peasants and agricultural labour was more diversified.[1] The latter tried to acquire more livestock to compensate for their lack of adequate land, and some of them even had a petty trade or business. Extracting firewood and selling it on headloads was another source of livelihood for them. This was a conspicuous feature particularly in Kangod Kansur which was closer to the highway than the other villages. However, they were reluctant to discuss this issue. The exact number of households engaged in this, or the income earned from this could not be assessed. Though

[1] This was an instance of diversification of the weak or 'forced diversification' as Rao called it. *Cf.* V.M. Rao, *Rural development and the village*. New Delhi: Sterling, 1980, p. 41. Such a diversification among the weak was also observed in a study of three drought prone districts in South India. *Cf.* M.V. Nadkarni, *Socio-economic conditions in drought-prone areas*, sponsored by the Central Water Commission, New Delhi. Concept, 1985, p. 104.

such extraction was mainly confined to minor and reserved forests, it was also carried out in private holdings with dry land having trees. On the one hand, it reflected a pressure to eke out a living in the face of inadequate land and alternative job opportunities. On the other hand, it reflected the pressure from the larger economy for fuel wood,since such activities were mainly observed in a village which was more 'open' than the others. However, the dependence of other classes in the higher levels of the rural hierarchy on the forests was no less exploitative as we shall soon see. The two higher classes had the lion's share of access to forest land. The class character of land use and control will be discussed later.

Land Use and Abuse

The locals depend on forests in several ways. The pressure on land leads to encroachment of forest land for extension of settlements and cultivation. This process is gradual and takes a long time, maybe even a decade. Though mainly the village or minor forests are used for this, the reserve forests are also used, though in a slow and phased manner. In the first phase, trees are gradually killed (through excessive cutting of branches, if not always through girdling), and forest land is converted into grassland which is later brought under cultivation. Second, forest lands are used for grazing, and when the grass cover of the nearby forests is depleted, grazing is extended into the interior. Third, branch wood is collected for fuel, both to meet subsistence needs of wood gatherers, as well as to sell it to households in the bigger villages and towns outside. Fourth, green manure is collected from forests—both from minor forests of the community and *bettas* under exclusive private control. Though households owning *bettas* are not supposed to exploit minor forests, it is not uncommon to find them doing so either to conserve their own *bettas*, or to supplement the inadequate produce of their already degraded *bettas*. Apart from these uses, locals also depend on the forests for their timber requirements—for housing, agricultural implements and fencing. Gathering minor forest produce like honey is increasingly rare. Though forests with abundant tree cover can indirectly help villagers by preventing quick siltation of tanks and streams, and by enriching water springs in their wells, such a collective use of forests somehow takes a low priority even if realised. The most urgent personal needs and direct benefits are assigned higher priority.

Being located in a forest region, villages in this region obviously would have more of their area under forests (legally defined) and less under cultivation than other villages. In the four villages covered, forest area accounted for 56 per cent of the land excluding *bettas* and 82 per cent including *bettas*. In contrast, net cultivated area accounted for only 11 per cent, ranging from 9 to 15 per cent across the villages. Apart from reserved forests and minor forests which are directly under the control of the government, the *bettas* are also officially considered as forest area but have really to be taken separately as they are under exclusive private use. When net cultivated area increased (as in Somanalli), it was mainly at the expense of government controlled forests, since the proportion of *betta* area also increased with cultivated area. There were no separate community or village controlled forests—apart from minor forests under the Forest Department, where villagers had a free access for the purposes of grazing and collecting fuel wood on headloads. The land use pattern in the four selected villages is presented in Table 7.2. The data on cultivated area, *benas* (grassland) and *bettas* are taken from the information collected from the questionnaires canvassed. They relate to area within the village.[2]

The settlement pattern in the villages is of a scattered nature. The residential plots and buildings are not concentrated in one place, and it is difficult to demarcate them from the agricultural area. The residences of gardeners have paved floors around them which are used for drying and processing arecanuts. But such areas as also areas occupied by buildings have been ignored here, since they account for a small proportion of the total village area or even total area under private control. As such, the data and proportions given in Table 7.2 are only broadly indicative of the magnitudes involved, and should not be taken as accurate measurements.

Before discussing land use, it is useful to take note of the human

[2] An enquiry with the village officials and others revealed that practically no area in these villages was under the control of non-residents. Even if formally owned by others, such area—quite marginal in magnitude—was under the control and operation of resident households only. As such, the difference between the total geographical area of the village and the total area privately controlled has been taken as area under government forests. Area under non-agricultural use like roads was quite small and therefore has been ignored.

Table 7.2 Village Land Use Patterns

Land Type	*Gadihalli*	*Somanalli*	*Kangod Kansur*	*Haldot*	*All Four*
1. Total area (acres)	969	563	434	390	2356
2. Net cultivated area (acres)	86	86	46	38	256
As % of (1)	8.9	15.3	10.6	9.7	10.9
a) Garden (acres)	30	38	17	17	102
As % of (1)	3.1	6.7	3.9	4.4	4.3
b) Paddy land (acres)	52	46	29	21	148
As % of (1)	5.4	8.2	6.7	5.4	6.3
c) Dry crops (acres)	4	2	—	—	6
As % of (1)	0.4	0.4	—	—	0.3
3. *Bena* (grass) land (private) (acres)	42	93	15	3	153
As % of (1)	4.3	16.5	3.5	0.8	6.5
4. *Betta* land (Revenue forest under private control) (acres)	172	206	152	87	617
As % of (1)	17.8	36.6	35.0	22.3	26.2
5. Other land under private control (acres)	9	5	1	2	17
6. Total land under private control = (2) + (3) + (4) + (5) (acres)	309	390	214	130	1043
As % of (1)	31.9	69.3	49.3	33.3	44.3
7. Forest land other than (4) including minor and reserved forests (acres)	660	173	220	260	1313
As % of (1)	68.1	30.7	50.7	66.7	55.7

Note: Public area under non-agricultural use like roads is ignored, being quite small. The difference between the total area of the village and the total land under private control is taken to be the area under forests.

pressure on land in the respective villages. These villages are sparsely populated, the population per square kilometre of the total village area (including forests) being only 40 in Gadihalli, 60 in Somanalli, 124 in Kangod Kansur, 49 in Haldot and 62 in all the four villages together. This density is far below that seen in villages in non-forest areas.[3] If, however, government controlled or public forests are excluded, the population per square kilometre of area in these villages is 126, 87, 246, 148 and 139 respectively, which brings them approximately on the same level as other villages. However, Kangod Kansur has far more

[3] Population per square kilometre in *rural areas* in 1981 was 78 in Uttara Kannada, 117 in Shimoga and 140 in Karnataka.

than the normal pressure on land, even compared to non-forest villages. It is not, therefore, surprising that forests around this village were far more degraded than in other villages. We may recall that in this village the extraction of fuel wood for sale as a source of earning was prominent, and the proportion of landless labour too was higher as compared to other villages. If the proportion of poor peasant households is added to that of landless labour, it amounted to a formidable 78 per cent, which is another indication of the high pressure on land here. Though the proportion of land under private control is even less in Gadihalli and Haldot than in Kangod Kansur (see Table 7.2), the pressure on land is less in the former two since the area in absolute terms is relatively more compared to the village population.

The pressure on land is also indicated by the size of an average holding, which is lowest in Kangod Kansur. The size of an average holding is larger in Gadihalli and Somanalli villages (of Sirsi taluk) than in the other two. The average size of holdings is given in Table 7.3 both with and without *bettas* for all villages and all classes of cultivating households. Since *bettas* account for a large part of privately operated holdings, the average size of a holding is considerably

Table 7.3 Average Size of Holdings (a) With and (b) Without *Bettas* (in acres) by Class of Households and Village Selected

Class of Households		*Gadihalli*	*Somanalli*	*Kangod Kansur*	*Haldot*	*All Four*
Landlords	a	28.7	40.1	81.8	40.1	43.6
	b	9.5	20.2	11.8	8.6	15.0
Capitalist	a	21.4	31.3	7.3	10.6	20.2
farmers	b	9.4	10.7	2.3	3.9	8.0
Middle	a	22.7	—	4.3	—	13.5
peasants	b	7.7		0.8		4.2
Poor	a	4.4	3.2	2.9	4.3	3.5
peasants	b	4.4	2.2	2.9	3.3	3.2
All cultivating	a	17.1	27.8	13.3	14.3	18.2
households	b	7.6	13.1	3.8	4.7	7.4

reduced if they are excluded. On the whole, each household has about 10 acres of *bettas* and there is not much variation between villages in this regard, though the variation between classes is significant. The average size of a holding excluding *bettas* is only as low as 3.8 acres in Kangod Kansur and goes up to 13.1 acres in Somanalli. However, the holdings are larger in this region than in the district as a whole.[4] The bulk of the holdings in the district cultivate paddy and are small and are mostly in the coastal areas where the pressure on land is maximum.

The average size of holdings in different classes can also be seen from Table 7.3. The landlords have the biggest holdings in all the villages and poor peasants the smallest. This disparity is particularly high in Somanalli.Since *bettas* are attached to gardens and gardens are usually owned by landlords, the inclusion of *bettas* only increases the disparity. The hold of the rural elite in villages is strengthened and consolidated further through their control over natural resources like *bettas*, which though not owned by them, are associated with the ownership of the most coveted lands.

The land under private control in the selected villages can be grouped into several categories: (a) garden land which is the most productive and commercialised of all land types/uses; (b) paddy land which is largely of subsistence nature; (c) other land under cultivation, consisting chiefly of dry crops like pulses and groundnut, or tree crops like mango, jack and cashew; (d) *bena* or grassland which is of a supportive nature, providing fodder for livestock of the households; and (e) *betta* land which is also of a supportive nature, providing leaf manure to areca gardens. Only the first three comprise cultivated areas. The proportion of area under gardens, paddy, *benas* and *bettas* is shown in Table 7.4, village-wise and class-wise. Since category (c) was insignificant in magnitude, land use under the remaining four types has been discussed.

In village agriculture, arecanut is the main commercialised crop, and all attention is concentrated on this. Along with areca, cardamom and pepper are cultivated as joint crops which are also commercialised. Though the area under gardens constituted only 4.3 per cent of the total area of the four villages taken together and 9.8 per cent of the land under private control, its role is far more dominant than is indicated by these proportions. It appears as if the whole physical and social environment has only a single purpose—to maintain the productivity of areca gardens. It is at the top of the 'food-chain' like a lion in a forest with the right to devour anything in his 'kingdom'. The green manure from *bettas* is used solely for areca gardens. The grass

[4] In 1980–81, the average size of a holding was 3.1 acre in this district, 5.2 acres in Shimoga district and 6.7 acres in Karnataka as a whole. *Cf.* Government of Karnataka, *Report of the findings of the agricultural census 1980–81*, State Agricultural Commissioner, Bangalore, 1985.

Table 7.4 Composition of Land Under Private Control—Class-wise, Village-wise (Percentages to total land holding including *bettas*)

Class of Cultivating Households	*Land Type*	*Gadihalli*	*Somanalli*	*Kangod Kansur*	*Haldot*	*All Four*
Landlords	ag	11.3	10.2	8.5	12.5	10.2
	pl	5.2	10.9	4.3	8.9	8.0
	bn	11.6	27.4	0.9	Nil	14.5
	bt	66.8	49.9	85.6	78.7	65.6
Capitalist farmers	ag	11.3	7.7	10.3	6.0	9.5
	pl	13.4	9.2	20.7	26.2	13.6
	bn	13.9	17.0	Nil	4.7	13.5
	bt	56.1	65.8	69.0	63.1	60.4
Middle peasants	ag	7.4	—	18.6	—	9.2
	pl	13.2	—	Nil	—	11.1
	bn	13.2	—	Nil	—	11.1
	bt	66.2	—	81.4	—	68.6
Poor peasants	ag	Nil	13.7	1.5	29.2	8.3
	pl	81.6	51.0	58.3	32.2	59.1
	bn	18.4	3.9	40.2	5.8	21.8
	bt	Nil	31.4	Nil	23.4	9.1
All cultivating households	ag	9.7	9.8	7.9	13.2	9.8
	pl	16.9	11.7	13.4	16.2	14.2
	bn	13.6	23.8	7.0	2.3	14.7
	bt	55.7	52.8	71.0	66.9	59.2

Note: ag is areca gardens; pl is paddy lands; bn is *bena*; bt is *betta*.
The proportion of land under other crops, fallows and cultivable wastes is not shown separately, which is the difference between 100 and the sum of the four land types shown. Fallows and cultivable wastes were negligible.

from *benas* is fed to livestock, and the bulk of livestock is maintained not for milk, but for the dung which is needed as farmyard manure for arecanut cultivation. Public forest areas are used for grazing during the day and cattle are led to the cowsheds only in the evenings. Garden cultivators collect every bit of dung and use it for areca gardens.

The same care is not given to other lands, including paddy lands. Green manure from *bettas* is not used for paddy lands even by households having *bettas*, since it is not enough to meet the needs of areca gardens. However, farmyard manure—including composted leaf manure—is used for paddy but this is more likely in the case of richer farmers who have *bettas, benas* and livestock. Such manure is very inadequate for the paddy lands of middle and poor peasants. Chemical fertilisers are not preferred since paddy is cultivated mostly as a single crop in the rainy season and fertilisers are likely to be washed away by the rain. Paddy lands are almost entirely rainfed, except for a few acres in Haldot; wherever irrigation is available it is used for raising gardens. In absolute size, paddy lands dominate, accounting for 57.8 per cent of the net cultivated area, compared to 39.8 per cent under areca gardens. Paddy is very important to the economy of poor peasants. Though on the whole, only 35.4 per cent of paddy lands were operated by poor peasants (compared to only 7.2 per cent of garden lands under them), 87.6 per cent of their cultivated area was under paddy (compared to only 12.4 per cent under gardens). As can be seen from Table 7.4, the proportion of garden land and *bettas* increases and that of paddy decreases the higher the position in the socio-economic hierarchy of classes.

The concentration of garden lands as well as *bettas* in the hands of landlords and capitalist farmers gives an advantage to them in paddy too. Taking all villages together, landlords obtained a yield of 1,358 kgs of paddy per acre while capitalist farmers obtained 1,239 kgs. In contrast, middle peasants obtained only 450 kgs and poor peasants 644 kgs per acre. The average yield for all classes and villages was 1,033 kgs per acre. Though the upper two classes together had a smaller share of paddy lands than of gardens, even this share was nearly 60 per cent though they constituted only 30 per cent of the households. The share of different classes of cultivating households in different types of lands can be seen from Table 7.5. It is interesting to observe that access to even government owned natural resources like *bettas* is determined by control over private land. Higher the share a class has in better endowed cultivated areas, the greater is its claim on the rest of resources including forests. This is so even in case of encroachments.

Both *benas* and *bettas* are on the upper reaches of the terrain, while paddy lands or gardens occupy lowlands and valleys. *Benas* are generally at a lower level than *bettas* close to the paddy lands. They are a source of grass, and also serve as private pastures after the grass is harvested during the dry season. Some of the cultivated lands including paddy lands were actually converted or developed from out of *bena* lands, and some of the present *benas* may as well be cultivated in future. Unlike *bettas*, *benas* are privately owned; where they are not, they are encroachments on the forests with the intention of eventually cultivating them either with paddy or with other crops like pulses and

Table 7.5 Share (per cent) of Classes of Cultivating Households in Different Types of Land

Share in Type of Land	*Share (per cent) of*			
	Landlords	*Capitalist Farmers*	*Middle Peasants*	*Poor Peasants*
Gadihalli				
Garden	32.4	56.4	11.1	Nil
Paddy	8.6	38.5	11.5	41.3
Bena	24.0	49.9	14.4	11.7
Betta	33.5	49.0	17.5	Nil
Total	28.0	48.7	14.7	8.6
*Somanalli**				
Garden	75.0	19.1	—	4.6
Paddy	66.9	18.9	—	14.2
Bena	82.3	17.1	—	0.5
Betta	68.0	30.0	—	2.0
Total	72.0	24.1	—	3.3
Kangod Kansur				
Garden	83.1	4.5	9.5	2.9
Paddy**	24.4	5.2	Nil	65.1
Bena	10.3	Nil	Nil	88.0
Betta	92.1	3.3	4.6	Nil
Total	76.7	3.4	4.0	15.0
Haldot				
Garden	58.8	11.2	—	30.0
Paddy	34.0	39.7	—	26.3
Bena	Nil	60.0	—	40.0
Betta	72.4	23.0	—	4.6
Total	62.1	24.6	—	13.3
All Four Villages				
Garden	61.1	26.3	4.9	7.2
Paddy	33.3	26.1	4.1	35.4
Bena	58.1	25.2	3.9	12.6
Betta	65.0	27.7	6.0	1.3
Total	58.7	27.2	5.2	8.5

Note: This can be compared with the class-wise share in number given in Table 7.1

* In this village, two service class households have 2.5 acres together, 0.5 acres of garden and 2 acres of grass land. This formed only 0.6 per cent of total land under private control.

** 1.5 acres, i.e., 5.3 per cent of village total is cultivated on lease by two service class households here.

groundnut. The forest officials believe that most *benas* were originally minor forests, which were heavily grazed, deforested and privatised. A few elderly respondents from *bena* owning households confirmed this, but such privatisation took place decades ago. In fact, and on their own admission, *benas* of some households have yet to be regularised and have no ownership titles. Though *benas* are grasslands, there was no evidence of a productive and systematic cultivation of grass. They are usually residual lands incidentally having grass. *Benas* are put on fire annually after harvesting to facilitate regrowth. The grass is of an inferior type, known locally as *karada*, which is not supposed to be nutritious for animals. Karada is also used for thatching roofs of hutments and for giving cover to erosion prone soil and for preventing the growth of weeds around areca trees. *Benas* do not even permit tree growth because of the practice of burning and subsequent grazing. There was no evidence of growing fodder trees by protecting them. *Benas*, however, contribute towards the survival of cattle which produce dung, if not milk.

The difference between *benas* on the one hand and fallows and cultivable wastes on the other is that the latter two were cultivated at one time or the other. Fallows and cultivable wastes, however, were negligible in the villages covered (see Table 7.2). *Benas* on the whole, constituted 15 per cent of the total landholdings inclusive of *bettas*, their proportion being larger in the villages of Sirsi taluk than in those of Siddapur taluk (see Table 7.4). That is, they constituted a smaller proportion where the pressure on land was greater. *Benas* were converted into cultivated areas here more than in the other two villages. Across classes, *benas* occupied a more prominent role among the poor peasants than among others, accounting for 22 per cent of the total land under their control. It is interesting to observe that the least productive of the four land types is relatively more concentrated among the poor peasants, thereby indicating how natural resources are distributed. They do not have other complementary resources to convert it into a more productive resource. Since richer farmers have the resources to bring these lands under cultivation, the poor peasants may eventually lose them to the rich. Only 12.6 per cent of the total *bena* land is shared by the poor peasants, while 58.1 per cent is shared by landlords, taking all the four villages together (see Table 7.5).

Not only do poor peasants have a low share in *benas*, their grass yield is also lower. This is because they cannot afford to protect their lands from grazing by stray cattle, which the richer farmers can afford.

Landlords and capitalist farmers have trenches and strong fences around both their *benas* and *bettas*. In villages where *benas* were under richer farmers, yields were higher. Thus, yields of grass per acre were 1,022 kgs in Gadihalli and 1,185 kgs in Somanalli, while the yields were only 859 kgs in Kangod Kansur and 880 kgs in Haldot. Class-wise yield differences as well as differences in the level of protection given to *benas* can be seen from Table 7.6. It may be noted that though as many as ten *benas* out of twelve under poor peasants were reported to be fenced, most of them had weak or nominal fencing mainly to demarcate the boundaries. There was no real protection against grazing by stray cattle, and their grass yield was lowest. We can thus observe how yields decline as we descend the social ladder from the landlord class.

Table 7.6 *Bena* Lands—Level of Protection, Size and Yield

(Class-wise, taking all the four villages together)

Class of Cultivators	*No. of* Benas					*Average Size of* Benas *(acres)*	*Gross Yield per Acre (kgs)*
	Total	*Fenced Only*	*Trenched Only*	*Both Trenched and Fenced*	*Neither Trenched nor Fenced*		
Landlords	9	1	1	7	Nil	9.8	1175
Capitalist farmers	10	8	1	1	Nil	3.8	1079
Middle peasants	1	1	Nil	Nil	Nil	6.0	1000
Poor peasants	12	10	Nil	Nil	2	1.6	864
Salaried service	1	1	Nil	Nil	Nil	2.0	1000

Betta lands or 'soppina bettas' are actually 'protected' forests assigned to garden lands. The privileges enjoyed by gardeners include collection of leaf manure and fodder, grazing cattle, erection of hutments and cattle sheds, digging water channels, sinking drinking water wells, storage of straw and other material, clearing and burning of weeds like lantana, and removal of earth, clay and stone. The *bettas*—when officially recognised—are cited in the title-deed of garden lands, so that when the latter change hands due to sale or inheritance, *bettas* attached with it also change hands but not independently of gardens.

The use of *bettas* is exclusive to their holders by title. Thus, *bettas* are almost as good a private property as gardens, but for certain restrictions and responsibilities imposed on *betta* holders. They cannot cut, damage or lop or in any way injure trees under the reserved category, without prior permission. Legally, tree stands (timber) are a property of the government, including trees planted, and not of the *betta* holders. The latter are also expected to maintain 100 trees per hectare in these lands, of which 50 per cent should be of the reserved variety. If the actual number of trees are less than this minimum, the *betta* user is expected to plant trees at his cost and maintain them. If this is not done, privileges can be suspended by the Forest Department. In practice, however, there has been no instance of any *betta* holder losing privileges when he violated the rules and left *bettas* in degraded state. Such degraded *bettas* are more common than the well maintained ones.

The number of trees are no indication of the state of health of *bettas*. The majority of *bettas* may have the officially specified minimum. However, due to excessive lopping of trees most of them look like skeletons, particularly in areas where the pressure on land is higher and other forests are also limited or degraded.[5] *Betta* users till recently did not even try to plant new trees that yield leaf manure. Today some efforts have been made to organise *betta* holders in terms of an informal association and induce them to grow more trees on their *bettas* and to protect their interests, yet such attempts are limited. For example, though these efforts including planting of trees on *bettas* were prominent in a nearby village Bhairumbe, the selected villages did not show evidence of much activity of this nature. Apart from not planting new trees, gardeners also cut *bettas* for soil to spread around areca trees as a cover over leaf manure. This soil mining has made several areas of *bettas* erosion-prone. Significantly, soil is removed only from *bettas* or minor forests, but not from their own *benas*.

Traditionally *betta* users were aware of the necessity for a sustainable

[5] We have not made any attempt to measure the extent of degradation of *bettas*. An earlier study, by Mani, of a village in Sirsi division tried to quantify it by taking some twelve indicators (trees per acre, mean girth of trees, mean height of trees, extent of vacant patches, grazing intensity, ground cover, soil erosion, etc.). It found that about 34 per cent of *betta* area was degraded by more than 50 per cent and 41 per cent of area by more than 30 per cent but less than 50 per cent. See Ajit Mani, 'Agrarian technology and eco-degradation of betta forests in Salkani, a village in North Kanara District', Technical Report, Centre for Ecological Sciences, Indian Institute of Science, Bangalore (Unpublished), esp. p. 26. Also see Table 5.3.

use of *bettas*, if not of the public forests around them. They demarcated *bettas* into two or three parts, which they rotationally exploited. As a result, trees were harvested for leaf manure only in alternate years. However, since artificial or manual planting of trees was insignificant and natural regeneration of new trees was constrained by grazing, the actual harvesting has been on the whole beyond sustainable limits. Unsustainable cutting has become a major problem because most of the harvesting is done by hired labourers, who do not differentiate and even cut apical shoots. Earlier, the gardeners themselves used to lop branches for leaf manure and made sure that further growth of trees was not unduly affected. Quite a few respondents felt that degradation in *bettas* has been continuing for decades and that it is not a recent phenomenon.

Some *bettas* are actually encroachments upon forests, and not lands officially granted to gardeners. Officially, *bettas* were granted in the past only for old areca gardens. No *bettas* were given for new gardens. However, some of the gardeners who developed new gardens went ahead and enclosed and attached parts of forest land to their gardens to harvest leaf manure, so as to prevent others from exercising similar privileges. This was conceded frankly by respondents, as it was an open secret in the villages. Estimates of such encroached *betta* lands (as a per cent of total *betta* land) under respective villages and classes of cultivators can be seen from Table 7.7. These estimates are based on the information given by the respondents. They expect the government to regularise their rights on these *bettas* as in the case of old gardens. It can be seen from the table that the proportion of encroached *bettas* increased steadily as one moves down the social class ladder, with poor peasants having acquired all their *bettas* through encroachments. It should also be noted that the poor peasants shared only 1.3 per cent of all *bettas* (see Table 7.5) and the bulk of the encroached *bettas* were under the control of landlords and capitalist farmers.

All areca gardens do not have proportionately the same extent of *bettas* in spite of additions made through encroachments. Across villages, the ratio varied from 5.1 acres of *betta* per acre of garden to 9.3 acres, and across classes from 1.1 acre in the case of poor peasant gardeners to 7.5 acres in the case of middle peasants (see Table 7.7). While the first three classes of households had more *bettas* in relation to gardens, the poor peasants had much less. On the whole, an acre of areca garden had 5.9 acres of *bettas*, which is less than the ratio of 1:9 permitted in the past. Thus, the disparity in the case of *bettas* was even more than in the case of garden lands. An extreme case of concentration

Table 7.7 *Bettas* and their Estimated Produce in a Year

	Betta *Land in Acres, per Acre of Garden Land*	*Per cent Encroached from Forests*	*Biomass harvested per acre of* Bettas *(in kgs)*				
			Green Leaves	*Dry Leaves*	*Dry Grass*	*Firewood*	*Total*
Village-wise							
Gadihalli	5.7	8.8	1288	1516	414	630	3848
Somanalli	5.1	28.2	2330	1516	34	491	4371
Kangod Kansur	9.3	7.9	454	236	218	164	1072
Haldot	5.1	11.5	892	377	287	356	1912
Class-wise							
Landlords	6.2	11.2	1383	1039	147	372	2941
Capitalist farmers	6.4	17.6	1340	1152	328	468	3288
Middle peasants	7.5	32.4	1378	486	486	730	3080
Poor peasants	1.1	100	925	656	60	750	2391
All villages and classes	5.9	15.4	1365	1032	216	426	3039

is seen in Kangod Kansur, where landlords have 83 per cent of garden land and 92 per cent of *bettas*.

Almost the same type of protection is given to *bettas* as to *benas*. On the whole, the quality of protection did not differ much between the first three classes. However, *bettas* of the poor classes did not have durable protection both because they were encroached lands and because of the general resource scarcity of the poor peasants.[6]

All *betta* lands are not similar in productivity. There is considerable variation both across villages and classes, as can be seen from Table 7.7. Leaf manure—both green and dry—is the major produce of *bettas*, followed by firewood. This is seen among all classes, but firewood has more significance for poor peasants than for the other classes. The total biomass extracted per acre is, however, the lowest among poor peasants mainly due to the fact that their *bettas* were already degraded before they encroached on them and acquired them. The biomass extracted is broadly indicative of the quality of *bettas*. The *bettas* in Somanalli were relatively well maintained and produced more than those in other villages, while *bettas* in Kangod Kansur were most degraded and produced the least. It may be recalled that Kangod Kansur has the highest degree of concentration in *bettas*, showing that exclusive private control is no insurance against unsustainable use. The lower extraction from *bettas* under landlords than among capitalist farmers and middle peasants is partly due to their efforts to limit extraction within sustainable limits. This is clearly evident from the fact that firewood extracted from *bettas* is lowest among landlords. Having the bulk of *bettas* under them, even a low rate of extraction per acre does not deprive them of the firewood needed to meet the requirements of their households. The total firewood obtained by them per household is much more than that obtained by other households. In the case of leaf manure, the needs of both landlords and capitalist farmers are almost insatiable, and some of their requirements are met through employing hired labour to fetch leaf manure—particularly dry leaf—from minor forests.

Bettas present a poignant example of a public natural resource privatised and cornered by the rural elite to fulfil the demands of a commercial crop that does not even meet the needs of nutrition. They

[6] Since we did not quantify the extent of *betta* degradation, it was not possible to rrelate the quality of *bettas* with their size or the size of holdings or the class of tivators. Mani's study for Salkani, however, found no correlation between the extent legradation and the size of *bettas*. If productivity is taken as an indicator of the ty of *bettas*, there was no such correlation in our study. *Ibid*., p. 27.

did not even serve as a buffer to check the pressure on minor forests, since they were far more degraded than the *benas*.[7] The privatisation and concentration of exclusive use of this public resource in the hands of a few households is basically objectionable.[8] Added to this is the fact that there is no machinery for monitoring the management of this resource in the public interest and in the interest of regeneration and sustainable use. If the Forest Department does not have the resources to takeover and manage them on environmentally sound lines and to meet the needs of the entire rural society, then the task should be assigned to a rural organisation evolved on co-operative lines representing all classes of households. Such an organisation, however, cannot be based on voluntary and free labour of poor peasants and agricultural labour alone, since they also face shortage of labour during the peak seasons.[9] Obviously they would have to be compensated for their labour, and yet have as equitable an access to *bettas* as the richer farmers. Ultimately, it is far more preferable for the village community to manage *bettas* equitably and on an environmentally sound basis.

Encroachments

Unofficial privatisation through encroachment of forests is another problem, which has already been noted in the context of *bettas*. This is not, however, the only form of encroachment, since encroached lands are used for cultivation as well. The bulk of encroached land is under the richer farmers—both landlords and capitalist farmers. Details of encroached land—its extent, percentage of encroached land under private control of different classes village-wise and also percentage share of each class in the total encroached land—are presented in Table 7.8. Details regarding the use of encroached land are given in Table 7.9.

[7] This is observed in Mani's study as well. *Ibid*., p. 26.

[8] Mani sheds light on why *betta* holders could not attend to regeneration of *bettas*. 'Any major forestry work (nursery to planting) in the villages would coincide with the peak period in areca and paddy field observations'. *Ibid*., p. 39.

[9] 'It is not reasonable to expect poor farmers who are suffering from an acute labour shortage to donate several hours to community forestry work each day'. *Ibid*., p. 39.

Table 7.8 Encroached Land—Its Extent and Class-wise Share

Class of Households		*Gadihalli*	*Somanalli*	*Kangod Kansur*	*Haldot*	*All Four*
Landlords	a	Nil	43	1	9	53
	b	Nil	15.3	0.6	11.5	8.7
	c	Nil	61.4	4.6	32.1	35.6
Capitalist farmers	a	18	15	5	8	46
	b	12.0	16.5	69.0	23.6	16.3
	c	62.1	21.4	22.7	28.6	30.9
Middle peasants	a	5	—	7	—	12
	b	11.0	—	81.4		22.2
	c	17.2	—	31.8	—	8.0
Poor peasants	a	6	10	9	11	36
	b	20.1	76.5	28.1	64.3	40.0
	c	20.7	14.3	40.9	39.3	24.2
All cultivating households	a	29	70*	22	28	149*
	b	9.3	18.0	10.3	21.5	14.3
	c	100	97.1	100	100	98.7

Note: a is in acres; b is encroached land as per cent of total land under private control; c is per cent share of the class in the total encroached land in the village.

* 2 acres of encroached land out of this was in the possession of a household under the salaried service class, used as grassland. This formed 80 per cent of the total land under its control.

Table 7.9 The Use of Encroached Land—Across Villages and Class of Cultivating Households

(per cent share of each use to total encroachment)

	Garden	*Paddy*	Bena	Betta	*Fallow*
Village-wise					
Gadihalli	Nil	19.3	28.1	52.6	Nil
Somanalli	6.0	5.7	Nil	82.6	5.7
Kangod Kansur	Nil	4.6	40.9	54.5	Nil
Haldot	10.0	41.4	7.2	36.0	5.4
Class-wise					
Landlords	4.3	7.5	Nil	84.4	3.8
Capitalist farmers	2.2	13.0	19.6	65.2	Nil
Middle peasants	Nil	Nil	Nil	100.0	Nil
Poor peasants	10.5	34.1	28.4	22.7	4.3
All villages and classes	*4.7*	*14.8*	*12.8*	*64.0*	*3.7*

The tables show that a higher proportion of land is encroached in Somanalli where forests and *bettas* are in a better state and pressure on land is not high, and encroachments are least in Kangod Kansur where both forests and *bettas* are highly degraded and pressure on land is greater. This may be partly because *betta* lands are less per acre of gardens in the former, providing a motivation for acquiring *bettas* through encroachments. Moreover, while the productivity or fertility of forest lands makes encroachment attractive, the dominant position of landlords and capitalist farmers makes it feasible. Though both in Somanalli and Kangod Kansur the bulk of land is under landlords and capitalist farmers, numerically these two classes of households together accounted for 46 per cent in the former (as against only 9 per cent in the latter), which seemed a favourable factor for effecting encroachments. Taking all the four villages together, 35.6 per cent of encroached land was accounted for by landlords, 30.9 per cent by capitalist farmers, totalling 66.5 per cent. In contrast, the land hungry poor peasants accounted for only 24.2 per cent. In Kangod Kansur and Haldot poor peasants are numerically more dominant, and therefore accounted for a higher per cent of encroached land.

It is also interesting to note that though the bulk of encroached land is under landlords and capitalist farmers, its proportion in the total land under their control is only 8.7 and 16.3 per cent respectively. Encroached land acquires more significance in the holdings of middle peasants (22.2 per cent) and even more in the case of poor peasants (40 per cent). What little land they have grabbed is a matter of survival for them.

Bettas are the major form of the use of encroached lands (64 per cent taking all villages together), particularly in Somanalli (83 per cent) which accounted for the major proportion of encroached lands, and among landlords and capitalist farmers who accounted for the bulk of encroachments. This clearly reveals that possessing *bettas* serves as a major motivation for encroachments, and if *bettas* are brought under common village management, a major source of encroachments of public lands would be plugged. Among the poor peasants, however, the most important use of encroached lands is for the cultivation of paddy (34.1 per cent), followed by their use as grasslands (28.4 per cent).

These encroachments, paradoxically, co-exist with the low cropping intensity of cultivated lands. Double cropping is insignificant, except in Haldot which enjoys the benefit of Aghanashini river flowing nearby. But even in this village only seven acres were under double cropping in paddy lands and gross cropped area as a ratio to net cropped area was a mere 118 per cent. This figure is not impressive though it is higher compared to other villages (101 in Gadihalli, 100 in Somanalli, and 104 in Kangod Kansur). No class-wise analysis of cropping intensity is meaningful when the overall cropping intensity is underestimated in a region dominated by garden crops, as these areas have crops all the year-round but are not counted among double cropped areas. There is some potential to raise cropping intensity in paddy lands. After the harvesting of paddy, the soil retains some moisture to raise pulses or groundnuts. However, this is not feasible as farmers are unable to control the menace of grazing by stray cattle. While this is effectively checked in the kharif season since the stakes are high and the loss through grazing can be considerable, it is not considered worthwhile to take this trouble in a season when productivity is both low and uncertain.

Fragmentation of Holdings and Cost of Fencing

Fragmentation of holdings is a common phenomenon in the district, especially in the case of areca gardens. Since lands differ in quality, each type of land is separately sub-divided and inherited so as to secure equitable inheritance. The problem arises in the case of *benas* and *bettas*, though occasionally they are jointly owned and operated. Such joint ownership between brothers and cousins is becoming rare even in the case of *benas* and *bettas*.

Generally the extent of fragmentation is higher than the size of holdings. This is so both across villages and classes of households as can be seen from Table 7.10. However, the average size of fragments is higher in the case of larger holdings, seen both across villages and classes. A small size overall holding constrains the extent of its fragmentation. It is thus clear from Table 7.10 that Kangod Kansur and Haldot, which have smaller holdings, have fewer numbers of fragments per holding and smaller fragments. Similarly, though landlords have the largest number of fragments per holding, the average size of their fragments is also the highest—over twelve times larger than those of poor peasants. On the whole, an average holding in the region has six fragments and the average size of each fragment is seventeen acres.

Fragmentation is not, however, perceived as a major problem by any household. On the other hand, an artificial attempt to ban fragmentation can give rise to intractable problems of equitable sharing by inheritors.

Table 7.10 Fragmentation of Holdings and Fencing Costs

	No. of Fragments per Holding	*Average Size of Fragment (acres)*	*Fencing cost per acre in Rs (including imputed cost of forest material and family labour used)*	
			Fixed	*Recurring*
Village-wise				
Gadihalli	7.6	17.1	39	7
Somanalli	9.9	24.5	114	29
Kangod Kansur	2.4	11.8	65	6
Haldot	2.8	11.7	34	9
Class-wise				
Landlords	11.4	43.7	85	15
Capitalist farmers	9.1	20.2	54	14
Middle peasants	4.7	13.5	35	9
Poor peasants	2.3	3.5	56	22
All villages and classes	*6.0*	*17.1*	*72*	*15*

Nevertheless, an important implication of fragmentation is the higher cost of fencing involved. Fencing is an important necessity in villages to guard against stray cattle and also to demarcate boundaries for indicating private property rights and to discourage petty thieving. Ordinarily, cattle holders are expected to keep a watch on their cattle and restrain them from straying into private properties. Theoretically, stray cattle can be impounded in village 'doddis' (pounds) and their owners penalised. However, each village does not have its own pound, and the burden of 'arresting' the stray cattle and taking them to pounds (normally ten to fifteen kms away) falls on the households onto whose property the cattle have strayed. Even after this, they are not compensated for the loss sustained.[10] Moreover, the village pounds are

[10] Wade has studied village conventions and institutions in regulating grazing in Kurnool district of Andhra Pradesh. Even here, there is no system of compensation by owners of straying cattle to victims of grazing. They are only penalised, the proceeds go

no substitute for fencing. Fencing is considered essential even where pounds function. Grazing on private property is considered a serious offence only if grazing takes place in spite of the fencing by pushing through and damaging the fence. As such, fencing is regarded as a necessity by all cultivating households. In a forest region like this, fencing does not involve any direct cash expenses, since almost all the material required is obtained from either *bettas* or minor forests. Thus, the cost of fencing is actually borne by the forests, except for a little expense involved in hiring labour.

The estimates of fencing cost per acre of holdings, both across villages and classes, are presented in Table 7.10. These costs include the imputed cost of family labour, as well as cash expenses on labour, the latter being a minor proportion. These costs are comparable across classes, since both hired labour and man-days of family labour (valued at market wages) are included. If hired labour alone was included, fencing costs incurred by poor peasants would have been underestimated. These costs are shown separately as fixed costs and recurring costs. Fixed costs relate to investments in erecting durable fences lasting more than a year, whereas recurring expenses relate only to repairs and maintenance costs and temporary fencing which lasts only a season. The imputed costs of forest based resources used in fencing here have not been separated, since the extent of forest dependence has been discussed separately.

The table suggests that though the number of fragments increases the cost of fencing, there is no smooth relation between these two because of the role of several other factors. Thus, even though the number of fragments is smaller in the case of Kangod Kansur and in the case of poor peasants on the whole, the per acre costs are higher in this village than in Gadihalli and Haldot, and higher among poor peasants than among capitalist farmers and middle peasants. In fact, recurring costs are highest in the case of poor peasants. In this case, the costs are not necessarily indicative of the quality and durability of fencing, but of the problems involved in securing resources. These problems increase when the average size of a holding is small, and when forests are degraded. The pressure of cattle on land also adds to

to village field guards and the council. There is no system of village managed field guards in the villages studied here. See Robert Wade, 'The management of common property resources: Finding a cooperative solution', *The World Bank Research Observer*, Vol. 2(2), July 1987, pp. 219–34, esp. 223–25.

the costs, since durable and stronger fencing is required. In the case of landlords however, the higher cost of fencing is indicative of durability and strength. By incurring the maximum investment on fencing (fixed costs) they also manage to get higher yields, which is not the case with poor peasants.

Chapter Eight

Arecanut Gardens and their Social Cost

The areca gardens occupy the most important position, not in terms of the area under gardens directly, but in terms of the demands on resources they make on the forests as we have seen earlier. The *betta* forests may have been privatised for exclusive exploitation but are nevertheless public property. This exploitation is not meant to meet the subsistence needs of a poor section of society, but to maintain the profitability of the highly commercialised economy of the local rich. The dependence on leaf manure from forests may have its own justification from the point of view of efficient cultivation of gardens. Thus, leaf manure not only serves as an organic manure, but also protects gardens from soil erosion—a very important function in an area with a heavy rainfall. Such dependence on leaf manure is far less significant in arecanut gardens in the Maidan areas. This is not only because they do not have leaf manure in such forest areas, but also because they are mostly irrigated and do not face the risk of heavy downpours for long periods which would lead to cutting of the soil and soil erosion. Even while conceding the necessity of abundant supply of leaf manure to arecanut gardens in the Western Ghats, we may try to assess the social cost of these gardens in the form of imputed cost of the resources drawn from the forests including the *bettas*. Such an assessment can give some idea of how huge private profits are made by the richest sections of rural society at public expense, and could lead to an awareness of the need for a better management of forest resources in the interests of all classes. One could also question whether such a social cost is justified for raising the crop which is not essential in meeting the nutritional needs of people.

The term 'social cost' is used in a narrow sense of the imputed cost of the use of public resources including *bettas*, and not in the wider sense of including a valuation of the cost in terms of deforestation, etc. For this purpose, we have taken into account three different types of costs separately: (a) *the private paid-out costs* which include wages paid to hired labour including labour hired for extraction of leaf manure, fertilisers, pesticides, purchased farmyard manure, purchased fuel wood for processing arecanut, interest on borrowed capital, water charges and taxes, and other cash expenses; (b) *imputed private costs* include the imputed cost of family labour valued at market wages;[1] and (c) *imputed social costs* which include the imputed value of leaf manure collected from *bettas* and other forests, fencing material collected from forests, fuel wood collected from forests for processing arecanut and farmyard manure.

It may be noted that farmyard manure is treated here as a part of the social costs but not as a part of the private imputed cost, because the bulk of fodder consumed by cattle comes from public resources as we shall see later. Grass from own farm is a small portion of the total fodder consumed by livestock. Moreover, the bulk of leaf manure in farmyard manure also comes from *bettas* and forests. To avoid double counting, only leaf manure directly applied is taken note of, since leaf manure added to farmyard manure is included in the value of the latter. The bulk of leaf manure extracted is actually directly applied.

There was a problem about the valuation of leaf manure because there is actually no market for it. However, there is a market for farmyard manure. In consultation with the Horticultural Department, we have treated one unit of farmyard manure as equal to two units of leaf manure by weight and valued the latter accordingly.

Uniform prices are assumed for the imputation for all the five villages so that differences in social costs are not on account of price differences and are comparable in real terms. However, the valuation of output and purchased inputs involves price differences depending on actual prices received or paid, but these price differences are not significant. The valuation of output includes supplementary or joint produce like pepper, cardamom, banana and coconut. Arecanut,

[1] Since bullocks are rarely used in gardens, the question of imputing the cost of their labour did not arise. Other farm raised material is not included in inputs because if it is included in inputs it has to be included in output as well. Some by-products like areca *sippe* (husk or cover), used as a fuel, are taken note of later. No areca gardens are leased in; no rents are paid, nor are they imputed. Similarly, no imputed interest on own capital is included.

however, accounts for the bulk of the produce. Data are based entirely on the respondents' replies which could not be physically verified. Some amount of underestimation of yields and income cannot be totally ruled out.

Details regarding the cost and returns per acre from areca gardens for the four villages in Uttara Kannada district and for Bharatipur in Shimoga district are presented in Tables 8.1 and 8.2 respectively. As can be seen from the tables, the imputed social costs accounted for one-third of the total cost in Uttara Kannada villages and 28 per cent in Bharatipur. Net return including social costs worked out to 235 per cent over the total costs, which is a huge margin of profits, taking the four Uttara Kannada villages together. If, on the other hand, social costs are excluded and only the first two categories of costs are included, then the net return would amount to 403 per cent over the total private costs. In Bharatipur, on the other hand, the net return over the total costs amounted to 241 per cent, while the net return exclusive of social costs amounted to 372 per cent. It may be recalled that we had covered Bharatipur village mainly as an example of a village where dependence on forest resources was much lower. We find, however, that there is a significant degree of dependence on forests even here, though lower than in Uttara Kannada villages. This is reflected both in the lower yield per acre of arecanut and also in the lower profit margin. The yields of arecanut given in the table relate to nuts after dehusking. The gardeners weigh them only after dehusking.

Interestingly, the proportion of social cost in the total cost does not vary significantly as between different classes, in spite of the variation in the ratio of *betta* lands to garden lands. Obviously, any inadequacy of *betta* lands is compensated by the garden owners through the exploitation of leaf manure from other forests. However, since garden lands are concentrated in the hands of landlords and capitalist farmers, to that extent the total demand on resources made by these two classes on the forests forms the lion's share.

Though in absolute terms total costs as well as social costs per acre do not vary much from class to class, both the gross and net returns vary and are in favour of the richer classes. The net returns per acre decline steadily as we move down the socio-economic ladder, and are positively correlated with the size of gardens. The larger gardens cultivated by the higher classes are more efficient. In Bharatipur, they are concentrated only in the first two classes, and there was not as much variation in the size of gardens here as in Uttara Kannada villages.

Table 8.1 Cost and Returns per Acre from Areca Gardens in the Four Villages of Uttara Kannada

	Private Paid-out Costs	*Private Imputed Cost*	*Imputed Social Costs*	*Total Costs*	*Gross Return**	*Net Return* including Social Cost*	*Net Return* excluding Social Cost*	*Yield** per Acre*
	Rs	*Rs*	*Rs*	*Rs*	*Rs*	*Rs*	*Rs*	*kgs*
Landlords	3410	—	1695	5105	18733	13628	15323	804
	(66.8)		(33.2)					
Capitalist farmers	3013	523	1759	5295	15832	10537	12296	734
	(56.9)	(9.9)	(33.2)					
Middle peasants	2350	1097	1702	5149	14102	8953	10655	687
	(45.6)	(21.3)	(33.1)					
Poor peasants	975	2138	1640	4753	10526	5773	7413	401
	(20.5)	(45.0)	(34.5)					
Total	3098	314	1706	5118	17169	12051	13759	753
	(60.5)	(6.1)	(33.3)					

Note: * Includes joint products like pepper.
** of arecanut after dehusking.
(Figures in brackets are percentages to total cost).

Table 8.2 Cost and Returns per Acre from Areca Gardens in Bharatipur (Shimoga)

	Private Paid-out Costs	*Private Imputed Cost*	*Imputed Social Costs*	*Total Costs*	*Gross Return**	*Net Return* including Social Cost*	*Net Return* excluding Social Cost*	*Yield** per Acre*
	Rs	*Rs*	*Rs*	*Rs*	*Rs*	*Rs*	*Rs*	*kgs*
Landlords	3873	—	1522	5395	18383	12988	14510	699
	(71.8)		(28.2)					
Capitalist farmers	3799	378	1561	5738	19562	13824	15385	737
	(66.2)	(6.6)	(27.2)					
Total	3839	174	1540	5553	18925	13372	14912	698
	(69.1)	(3.1)	(27.7)					

Note: * Includes joint products like pepper.
** of arecanut after dehusking.
(Figures in brackets are percentages to total cost).

There are several factors which account for the higher efficiency of larger gardens and richer classes: their advantage in the market associated with the large size of produce enabling them to have better terms; better processing of arecanut enabling them to get higher prices; increased ability to raise supplementary or joint crops like pepper and cardamom; and higher overall efficiency in conducting operations adequately and in time.

It has often been suggested that farmers should use more chemical fertilisers and reduce their dependence on leaf manure because of the social cost involved and the resultant deforestation. The gardeners, however, believe that fertilisers are no substitute for leaf manure. They believe that even if fertilisers are used, it is absolutely necessary to use leaf manure in a region with a heavy rainfall. Of the forty-two gardens in the four villages in Uttara Kannada, only fifteen used chemical fertilisers[2] and there was no systematic difference between the yield of farmers using fertilisers and those who did not use them.[3] Capitalist farmers' using chemical fertilisers in their gardens were successful in obtaining higher yields (by 8 to 10 per cent).

While conceding the need for leaf manure in heavy rainfall regions, it may justifiably be asked why gardeners should not be charged for the use of this resource (on the basis of the imputed value of use), which in any case they are not contributing to regenerate. Moreover, since it is a scarce resource equally needed by paddy growing peasants, could not there be a more equitable system of sharing this resource?

[2] None of the seven gardeners in the poor peasants class used fertilisers. However, in the other three classes, half of the gardeners used them.

[3] On the whole, taking all the villages and classes together, while the arecanut yield in gardens using fertilisers was 752 kgs per acre, it was 753 kgs in others. No firm relationship could be established on the basis of our data between fertiliser use and yield.

Chapter Nine

Livestock Economy and its Social Cost

Forests play an important role in supporting and subsidising the livestock economy of the region. It cannot be said, however, that livestock plays a greater role in a forest region than elsewhere. Because of the greater role played by agricultural wastes in supplying fodder in other regions, the density of livestock population is actually higher there. Thus, while in Karnataka as a whole, the density of cattle and buffaloes together (including calves) per square kilometre of area was seventy-five in 1983, it was only forty-five in Uttara Kannada. In Shimoga district, however, it was higher at ninety-one. The greater role of paddy lands and the larger proportion of grazing areas in the latter district seem to have favoured higher density. Thus, the dependence of the livestock economy on the forests is much greater in Uttara Kannada than elsewhere. Within Uttara Kannada, however, the density is higher in the up-ghat forest region than in the coastal region, though paddy is relatively more important in the latter region. The inadequacy of grazing lands and forests, and the small size of paddy holdings in the coastal region are not the only factors responsible for this. The demand for livestock as a source of farmyard manure is more in the up-ghat region to meet the needs of its gardens.

Cattle in this region are almost invariably of a 'non-descript', short statured and inferior breed. Their fodder requirements are limited and depend on grazing for survival. Their milk yields are extremely low. Actually, buffaloes are the main source of milk. As such, while the working bullocks and buffaloes are given feed concentrates and a superior variety of purchased and home produced fodder, the other cattle depend on grazing and inferior varieties.

In the four villages covered here, the density of cattle and buffaloes per square kilometre of village area (including forests) was 69 overall

(50 in Gadihalli, 105 in Somanalli, 78 in Kangod Kansur and 55 in Haldot). This suggests that privatised forests, more than the forests under public control, support the livestock economy. However, for households which do not have such privatised forests, the other forests are the major source of sustenance for their livestock. But, as we shall see, they are not the major owners of livestock.

Details of livestock owned, village-wise and by different classes of households are presented in Table 9.1. Cattle account for the bulk of livestock, followed by buffaloes. Sheep and goats are insignificant and owned only by the agricultural labour which were acquired by them in recent years mostly under the anti-poverty programmes and through bank loans. Using the plea that sheep and goats are most harmful to forests and grazing by them cannot be easily controlled, the Forest Department is reported to have persuaded the local banks in the region not to give any more loans for acquiring such animals. Poultry are raised chiefly by poor peasants and agricultural labour, for which, however, bank loans are not discouraged. The table also gives the percentage share of different classes of households in the village totals of each type of livestock. While poor peasants account for the larger share of bullocks, the bulk of cattle and buffaloes are accounted for by the two richest classes.

The disparity in the livestock held can also be seen from the last column of the table. It is almost perfectly and positively correlated with the size of landholdings. A landlord household owns nearly 18 heads of livestock on an average, with the figure declining consistently and reaching a low of 1.8 in the case of agricultural labour households at the other extreme.

In estimating the fodder consumption by livestock, we have depended on the parameters given in a study by Rajapurohit.[1] According to him, in an effective grazing season of six months, an adult bovine (cows, bullocks and buffaloes) in a forest region consumes 12 kg per day on an average through free grazing. We have assumed that a calf (either cattle or buffalo) consumes 3 kg per day in the same season, and that stall-feeding to buffaloes and working bullocks is in addition to what they graze. We have also assumed that sheep and goats consume the same amount of fodder through grazing as do the calves of cattle and buffaloes (3 kg per day). However, in the lean season

[1] A.R. Rajapurohit, 'Bovine feed availability and requirement in Karnataka with reference to dairy development programmes', *Indian Journal of Agricultural Economics*, Vol. 30 (3), July–September 1975.

Table 9.1 Livestock Owned (Number) and Class-wise Share

Villages/Classes	*Bullocks**		*Cows**		*Buffaloes**			*Sheep and Goat*	*Poultry*	*Cattle and Buffaloes including Calves*	
	Total	*Working*	*Total*	*Milch*	*Total*	*Milch*	*Working*			*Total*	*Per Household*
(1)	*(2)*	*(3)*	*(4)*	*(5)*	*(6)*	*(7)*	*(8)*	*(9)*	*(10)*	*(11)*	*(12)*
Gadihalli	47	29	66	12	31	23	Nil	35	22	196	7.3
Somanalli	43	38	62	6	38	19	2	Nil	46	239	10.9
Kangod Kansur	28	28	29	7	32	20	Nil.	Nil	81	137	4.3
Haldot	13	12	33	5	21	8	6	Nil	32	87	7.9
Landlords	35 (26.7)	30 (28.0)	71 (37.4)	4 (13.3)	53 (43.4)	25 (35.7)	6 (75.0)	Nil	Nil	247 (37.5)	17.6
Capitalist farmers	29 (22.1)	27 (25.2)	48 (25.3)	12 (40.0)	22 (18.0)	17 (24.3)	2 (25.0)	Nil	12 (6.6)	137 (20.8)	9.8
Middle peasants	2 (1.5)	2 (1.9)	13 (6.8)	2 (6.7)	6 (4.9)	4 (5.7)	Nil	Nil	Nil	31 (4.7)	7.8
Poor peasants	63 (48.1)	46 (43.0)	47 (24.7)	8 (26.7)	18 (14.8)	12 (17.1)	Nil	Nil	55 (30.4)	181 (27.5)	7.2
Agricultural labour	2 (1.5)	2 (1.9)	11 (5.8)	4 (13.3)	20 (16.4)	10 (14.3)	Nil	35 (100)	114 (63.0)	54 (8.2)	1.7
Others	Nil	Nil	Nil	Nil	3 (2.5)	2 (2.9)	Nil	Nil	Nil	9 (1.4)	2.3
All villages and classes	131 (100)	107 (100)	190 (100)	30 (100)	122 (100)	70 (100)	8 (100)	35 (100)	181 (100)	659 (100)	7.2

Note: *Above 3 years old.
(Percentages in parenthesis).

during the remaining part of the year, it is assumed that adult cattle and buffaloes consume only 6 kg per day through grazing and goats and sheep consume only 1 kg per day. It may be noted, however, that to compensate for the inadequate consumption during the ineffective grazing season, working bullocks, milking cows and buffaloes are stall-fed. Discussions with the professional members of the veterinary department in the region, confirmed the reasonableness of these parameters.

The costs and returns from livestock, village-wise and class-wise are presented in Table 9.2. The costs relate only to fodder and exclude the cost of labour, hired or own. The costs of fodder correspond to paid-out or cash expenses, the imputed value of farm produced fodder (including grass from *benas*), and the imputed social cost. The imputed social cost is the imputed value of fodder consumed by livestock through free grazing, including an estimate of fodder from *bettas*. It excludes, however, the social cost imposed on society by free grazing in the form of expenses involved in fencing.[2] On the returns side, we have estimates of the output of milk (including consumption at source and sale), and the value of dung.[3] No estimate of the value of bullock and buffalo labour is included here.

The table shows that an overwhelming proportion of the total fodder costs, viz., 67 per cent on the whole, is accounted for by free grazing, indicating the enormity of dependence on forests. Though in absolute terms the richer sections of rural society—landlords and capitalist farmers—exploit forests far more than the poorer classes, in relative terms the dependence on forests is vital to the survival of the livestock economy of poor peasants and agricultural labourers, particularly the former. While 59 per cent of the fodder cost was accounted for by free grazing in the case of landlords and 56 per cent in the case of capitalist farmers, the percentage was as high as 89 per cent in the case of poor peasants and 72 per cent in the case of agricultural labourers. Understandably, the relative dependence of the service class on free grazing is highest, viz., 90 per cent. Purchased fodder accounts for only 10 per cent in their case, in contrast to 28 per cent in the case of agricultural labour.

[2] As noted earlier in Chapter 7, not all the cost of fencing can be attributed to stray cattle. Fragmentation of holdings also adds to this cost. Moreover, fencing is considered to be a necessity to demarcate boundaries and to indicate private control.

[3] Since farmyard manure is composed of both leaf manure and dung, only half of the value of manure is attributed to dung and included here.

Table 9.2 Fodder Costs and Returns from Livestock per Household

Village/Class	*Fodder Costs*				*Returns*			*Net Returns Excluding Cost (3)*	*Net Returns Including Cost (3)*
	Paid-out Cost	*Private Imputed Cost*	*Imputed Cost of Fodder Through Free Grazing*	*Total Cost*	*Milk*	*Dung*	*Total*		
	Rs (1)	*Rs* (2)	*Rs* (3)	*Rs* (4)	*Rs* (5)	*Rs* (6)	*Rs* (7)	*Rs* (8)	*Rs* (9)
Gadihalli	964	138	1960	3062	1463	268	1731	629	−1331
Somanalli	670	229	2420	3319	1467	274	1741	842	−1578
Kangod Kansur	483	105	1009	1597	1278	223	1501	913	− 96
Haldot	627	512	2104	3243	1818	402	2220	1081	−1023
Landlords	2425	439	4132	6996	4184	611	4795	1931	−2201
Capitalist farmers	1423	546	2487	4456	2244	493	2737	768	−1719
Middle peasants	358	Nil	1881	2239	1590	354	1944	1586	− 295
Poor peasants	74	157	1812	2043	834	206	1040	809	−1003
Agricultural labour	187	2	475	664	436	72	508	319	− 156
Service	40	Nil	351	391	488	144	632	592	241
All villages and classes	686	193	1757	2636	1442	270	1712	833	− 924

If the imputed cost of fodder consumed through free grazing is included in the total cost, all classes of households apart from the salaried and all the villages are found to be making substantial losses. It is the dependence on free grazing which makes the livestock economy viable. In other words, the basically non-viable cattle are profitable to them only because they are subsidised by forest dependence. If the costs imposed by livestock in the form of increased cost of fencing and the cost in terms of foregone second crops due to difficulties of fencing in the rabi season are to be included, the social costs of livestock dependence on free grazing could be considered immensely high.

It is paradoxical that in spite of the vital role played by grazing lands in supporting the livestock economy, they are poorly managed and the village community shows little interest in making these lands more productive and sustainable. Probably, both the size and quality of livestock adjust to fodder availability. Any effort to bolster up the livestock economy, either through dairy programmes or through goat and sheep rearing programmes, would certainly make it necessary to raise the quantity and quality of fodder from grazing lands, *bettas* and *benas*.

Chapter Ten

Forest Dependence—A Total View

In the two preceding chapters, the dependence on forests has been brought out in the case of two important activities of the households in monetary terms. Here a total view of the forest dependence of households is taken encompassing all activities, both in physical and monetary terms. The extent of forest dependence in physical terms per household in the case of fuel wood consumption, consumption of grass and straw, mulch and manure, fencing material and timber used for construction and repair during 1985–86, the reference year for our survey, is shown in Table 10.1. The figures relate basically to extraction, but there were no reports of noteworthy sale or disposal in kind, so that overall extraction matched consumption. *Bettas* as a source of extraction have been separated from forests in the table. However, since they are actually public owned forests, the extraction from *bettas* should be taken together with other forests to assess forest dependence. For purposes of comparison, the table shows extraction from own land including *benas* though *benas* have mostly been encroachments of forests either recently or in the past.

The first part of the table relating to fuel wood consumption shows that the consumption of fuel wood is significantly higher per household in the case of the two richest classes, and declines gradually as one moves down the class ladder. Fuel wood is actually regarded as a free commodity by almost all classes. Even the service class has depended entirely on the forests to meet its fuel wood needs. On the whole, 95 per cent of fuel wood consumption is met either from forests or from *bettas* (78 per cent from forests and 17 per cent from *bettas*) and only 5 per cent is met from own land. The proportion of fuel wood from own land is obviously zero in the case of agricultural labour and only 0.6 per cent in the case of poor peasants. In two villages, viz., Somanalli and Haldot, all the fuel wood is obtained either from forests or from *bettas*. Interestingly, there is considerable variation in fuel wood consumption as between villages, with Gadihalli and Somanalli having much higher rates of consumption than the other two. The variations correspond more or less to the differences in the level of degradation of public forests if not *bettas*. Forests around the former two villages in Sirsi taluk are on the whole better and more exploitable. Consumption seems to adjust to supply available.

Fuel wood consumption is 7.9 tonnes per annum per household, which appears to be on the higher side. Even on a per capita basis, fuel wood consumption is 1.18 tonnes taking all the classes and villages together, reaching a high of 1.8 tonnes in the case of capitalist gardeners and 1.4 tonnes in the case of other landlords. In contrast the per capita consumption of capitalist farmers without any gardens and depending mainly on paddy is only 0.6 tonnes. On the whole, gardeners have a much higher consumption level, without a corresponding interest in regenerating firewood production.

Such a high consumption level in the region can be explained by the fact that fuel wood is considered as a free good and there is no attempt to economise on its use. The gardeners require fuel wood for arecanut processing as well. Though arecanut husk can also be used for this purpose, yet firewood is preferred. Areca husk is used mainly for bath water heating, but fuel wood is also used significantly for this purpose. In almost all the households, particularly in the first three classes, bath water heating is an important use and accounts for a large proportion of fuel wood consumption. Big copper and iron vessels which can hold between ten to twelve buckets of water are heated throughout the day and many people are in the habit of taking a hot water bath twice a day even during summer. Some of the elderly people reported that earlier locals used even rosewood and nandi as a fuel in the rainy season, as its fire lasted longer and had better heating qualities compared to other woods.

Though the use of fuel efficient chulas designed by Astra have been canvassed for quite time, the traditional chulas still dominate. Only three households (two landlords and one capitalist farmer) out of ninety-two in the region use fuel efficient Astra chulas. Only four households from the landlord class have bio-gas plants. Two households (one landlord and one capitalist farmer) reported using kerosene stove and one household (landlord) an electric heater for cooking purposes. Thus, nearly 96 per cent of the households depend exclusively on traditional chulas which are not found to be fuel efficient. There is not much incentive for installing bio-gas plants because the

Table 10.1 Extent of Forest Dependence per Household

Village/Class	Fuel Wood Consumption (tonnes)				Grass and Straw (tonnes)				
	From Forests	From Betta	From Own Land*	Total Fuel Wood	From Forests	From Betta	From Benas	Paddy Straw	Total Grass and Straw
Gadihalli	7.53 (74.9)	1.64 (16.3)	0.88 (8.8)	10.05 (100)	19.60 (68.9)	2.59 (9.1)	1.58 (5.6)	4.67 (16.4)	28.44 (100)
Somanalli	6.93 (75.9)	2.20 (24.1)	0	9.13 (100)	24.20 (70.7)	0.32 (0.9)	5.03 (14.7)	4.69 (13.7)	34.24 (100)
Kangod Kansur	5.26 (87.8)	0.39 (6.5)	0.34 (5.7)	5.99 (100)	10.09 (71.5)	1.00 (7.1)	0.39 (2.8)	2.64 (18.7)	14.12 (100)
Haldot	4.14 (69.5)	1.82 (30.5)	0	5.96 (100)	21.01 (63.9)	2.18 (6.6)	0.20 (0.6)	9.49 (28.9)	32.88 (100)
Landlords	4.97 (46.6)	4.81 (45.1)	0.89 (8.3)	10.67 (100)	41.32 (65.5)	4.21 (6.7)	7.42 (11.8)	10.09 (16.0)	63.04 (100)
Capitalist farmers	8.71 (70.2)	2.79 (22.5)	0.91 (7.3)	12.41 (100)	24.86 (57.7)	4.00 (9.3)	2.95 (6.8)	11.27 (26.2)	43.08 (100)
Middle peasants	2.50 (30.3)	3.63 (43.9)	2.13 (25.8)	8.26 (100)	18.88 (67.7)	4.50 (16.1)	1.50 (5.4)	3.00 (10.8)	27.88 (100)
Poor peasants	6.69 (96.8)	0.18 (2.6)	0.04 (0.6)	6.91 (100)	18.10 (78.5)	0.02 (0.1)	0.66 (2.9)	4.28 (18.6)	23.06 (100)
Agricultural labour	5.83 (100)	0	0	5.83 (100)	4.76 (100)	0	0	0	4.76 (100)
Service	5.00 (100)	0	0	5.00 (100)	3.40 (98.3)	0	0.06 (1.7)	0	3.46 (100)
All villages and classes	6.19 (78.1)	1.36 (17.1)	0.38 (4.8)	7.93 (100)	17.56 (69.2)	1.45 (5.7)	1.82 (7.2)	4.55 (17.9)	25.38 (100)

Village/Class	*Mulch and Manure (tonnes)*			*Fencing Material from Forests (tonnes)*	*Wood Used for Construction and Repair (CFT) from Forests*
	From Forests	*From* Betta	*Total*		
Gadihalli	12.37 (41.0)	17.82 (59.0)	30.19 (100)	1.39	0
Somanalli	32.54 (47.5)	35.98 (52.5)	68.52 (100)	2.39	0
Kangod Kansur	12.03 (78.6)	3.28 (21.4)	15.31 (100)	0.50	0.80
Haldot	32.55 (76.4)	10.04 (23.6)	42.59 (100)	1.50	0
Landlords	85.40 (55.1)	69.67 (44.9)	155.07 (100)	2.86	0
Capitalist farmers	27.41 (47.1)	30.77 (52.9)	58.18 (100)	3.02	0
Middle peasants	11.01 (39.0)	17.24 (61.0)	28.25 (100)	2.05	0.25
Poor peasants	6.49 (92.7)	0.51 (7.3)	7.00 (100)	1.20	1.00
Agricultural labour	0	0	0	0	0.06
Service	1.89 (100)	0	1.89 (100)	0.55	0
All villages and classes	19.49 (54.7)	16.17 (45.3)	35.66 (100)	1.33	0.30

Note: * It includes mainly areca husk.
Figures in the brackets are the percentages to total in each type of material).

fixed capital needed for such plants is not considered worthwhile when fuel wood can be obtained free of cost. For the same reason, cash expenses on much cheaper Astra chulas are also grudged. On the whole, there is no feeling of any crisis on the fuel wood front in this region as yet. This is so even in the poor households, whose consumption of fuel wood is much lower. They seem to get what they need without too much trouble. This observation cannot, however, be generalised to all the villages, not even to all the villages in Uttara Kannada.

We have already taken note of the overwhelming importance of forests including *bettas* in the case of fodder and leaf manure and the lion's share enjoyed by the two richer classes. Table 10.1 presents the physical dimension of the picture. Grass and straw shown here includes that used for thatching roofs and for covering soils in arecanut gardens. The table also gives an estimate of wood consumed for fencing and for construction and repair during one year.

We may take an aggregative view of dependence of locals on forests which necessitates taking into account the contribution of forest produce to incomes generated. The major significance of forest produce to locals lies in the fact that it supports local economic activities and provides fuel and timber free of cost. The gain from forests by way of wages earned through direct employment has been negligible in the villages covered. Though forest nurseries and plantations have been set up in the region and the Forest Department has created other direct employment opportunities, their role continues to be marginal and there is little evidence of direct employment benefit in the villages covered. On the basis of information obtained from the local officers of the Forest Department, it was found that approximately 490 man-days of employment were generated per acre when minor forests were taken up for plantation and soil conservation. This is one-time employment and not of a continuing or regular type. Our purpose here, however, is to assess the imputed income from forest produce through the extraction of leaf manure, fuel wood, grass, fencing material and timber including an estimate of grass consumed by animals while free grazing. The wage income earned by poor peasants and agricultural labourers through casual labour hired out to the Forest Department, is included under wages. The imputed income from forest produce includes a valuation of the extraction from *bettas* as they are owned by the government, but not from *benas* which are considered to be private property.

While aggregating the income of households from different sources, care has been taken to avoid double counting. While taking into account individual economic activities like gardening or economics of a particular crop, the imputed cost of family labour and also farm produced inputs used in these activities has to be taken on the cost side. However, family labour and farm produced inputs are also outputs of the household, and as such constitute a source of imputed income accruing to it. This should be clear from the fact that if family labour or farm produced inputs had been sold, they would have been explicit sources of cash income. This imputed income, however, is cancelled out by the imputed cost, as they are used also as inputs. Thus, in the process of aggregating the income of households, the imputed cost of family labour and the value of farm produce like dung, and grass from *benas* are excluded here. This means that while computing the net income from cultivation and animal husbandry, only paid-out or cash expenses on inputs have been deducted from the value of output and not the imputed costs. The imputed valuation of forest produce extracted by households is added to the income from other sources to estimate the total income, because in the absence of such free access they would have had to pay for the same and the net income would have been to that extent less, assuming that they would have purchased the total quantity they extracted. It is possible to argue that in such a case they would not have purchased this quantity, though for accounting purposes an imputed value could nevertheless be taken to assess the role of such free access.

The total income per household, village-wise and class-wise, accruing from different sources is presented in Table 10.2. The table also gives the proportion of imputed income from forest produce as a percentage of the total income of the household. Agricultural labourers are the poorest in terms of per household income, though on the basis of per capita income, poor peasants are the poorest. The per household income of a landlord family is nearly ten times higher than that of an agricultural labour household, while the income of a capitalist farmer household is more than four times higher.

What is interesting here is that in absolute terms, the imputed income from forests is in the same order as the total income per household, both village-wise and class-wise except for a slight aberration in the case of the salaried service class. It indicates a high positive correlation between income and forest dependence. Landlords have the highest income from forests followed by capitalist farmers, middle

Table 10.2 Total Net Income per Household (in Rs) According to Class of Farmers

Village/Class	*From Agriculture and Animal Husbandry*	*Wage Labour*	*Other Sources*	*Imputed Income from Forest Produce*	*Total Income*	*Per Capita Income*
	Rs	*Rs*	*Rs*	*Rs*	*Rs*	*Rs*
Gadihalli	16820	3623	1327	4427(16.9)	26197	4476
Somanalli	25659	2730	995	6249(17.5)	35633	5681
Kangod Kansur	9859	4194	1814	2320(12.8)	18187	2732
Haldot	25404	3182	2182	4699(13.2)	35467	5002
Landlords	72644	0	2643	11906(13.7)	87193	12771
Capitalist farmers	28483	0	2886	6537(17.2)	37906	5706
Middle peasants	16037	0	1125	3799(18.1)	20961	3884
Poor peasants	4923	3749	206	2853(24.3)	11731	1535
Agricultural labour	249	7449	155	1058(11.9)	8911	1664
Service	710	600	7475	956 (9.8)	9741	2164
All villages and classes	17539	3555	1519	4163(15.5)	26776	4197

Note: Figures in brackets are percentages to total income.

peasants and poor peasants and agricultural labourers the least. In proportionate terms, however, among the cultivating households the percentages are in the reverse order. While the landlords receive about 14 per cent of their income from forests, the poor peasants receive 24 per cent from forests. However, even this has not helped in reducing the disparity in total incomes that otherwise prevails in agriculture. Though in relative terms, forests are more important to the smaller households with tiny holdings, this relieving feature is not seen in the case of agricultural labourers. It would appear that the ability of any class to take advantage of common property resources like forests depends very much on what other private productive assets they possess. The only way the assetless can gain from forests is through fuel wood consumption.

On the whole, forests account for nearly 15.5 per cent of the income. While this percentage may not appear to be very large, it is not insignificant either. It indicates that, contrary to common belief, people in rural households are not yet alienated from forest dependence in spite of the regulations governing the access to forests. The dependence on forests for leaf manure and fodder particularly is still the main source of sustenance of the local economy apart from the dependence for fuel wood. Thus, the contribution of forests to the local economy can be said to be much more than what is indicated by the proportion of the imputed value of forest extraction to the total income.

The irony of the situation is that even this substantial dependence and stake in forests has not stimulated significant efforts at regeneration and raising the productivity of forests among the locals. In spite of the fact that the selected villages were in the vicinity of Salkani village from where the Appiko movement was launched, there was not much evidence of a zeal for regeneration of degraded forests. The real factor leading to the alienation of people from forests, if and when it finally comes, will be the degradation caused by this apathy rather than the lack of access. There was not much evidence of any rigorous check on this access. The major reason for this apathy seems to be the acute class differentiation in the local economy, giving rise to unequal benefits from forests, and the lack of any communitarian institution to make a sustainable use of them. The study has also shown that even private and exclusive access to forests, as in the case of *bettas*, has not ensured their sustainable use. What was scarce from the point of the society as a whole and from a long-term perspective, was not equally scarce in the eyes of the richer sections of society who enjoyed the lion's share of benefits from the forests. No initiative or leadership can be forthcoming from other classes to regenerate and make a sustainable use of forests, as these classes are basically disadvantaged in taking such a lead.

The picture may appear to be rather dismal, particularly since a number of scholars have pointed out the creative potential of local people in taking care of the natural resources through evolving proper institutions. There are examples within Uttara Kannada itself where people even today have shown enthusiasm for taking constructive steps to regenerate *bettas* and minor forests, as has been the case in Bhairumbe village, in the Sirsi division. Yet, the field impression not only in the selected villages but also in general in the district and elsewhere is that such examples are, at present, more an exception than a rule. Moreover, even where such instances have been found, the efforts have been mainly such as to benefit the richer sections rather than the community as a whole. Projects to develop *bettas* are a case in point. These projects involve no radical steps such as to hand over *bettas* to new collective or communitarian institutions. The fear of even well meaning activists in the region that such radical attempts are bound to fail in regenerating *bettas* are also not unfounded. Attempts at regeneration, therefore, have been broadly within the existing institutional framework, without disturbing private property rights.

There is another implication of our analysis of the intra-local political economy, which can be disturbing to populists. It is taken for granted that commercial interests responsible for deforestation are to be found only in the larger economy, identified almost exclusively with industrial interests. But we find that the local rich, the areca gardeners, are highly commercialised and make huge profits by using forest resources free of cost. The dichotomy between the larger and the local economy in terms of profit versus subsistence, made by populists, loses its sharpness and meaning in this context. These gardeners are as much a part of the resource using larger economy as the industrial interests. Though one could still argue that their use of forest resources is not ecologically as destructive as the use by industries, we cannot ignore that they have shown no more interest in regeneration than modern industries.

Appendix to Part II

The prices used in the valuation of forest and farm produce which were not marketed are indicated here. The general principle was to impute prices which the users of such produce would have been prepared—or would have had—to pay if they were to purchase the same quantities.

Farm yard manure Rs. 40 per cart load to 500 kg approximately.

Leaf manure (green or dry) Rs. 40 per tonne
(A *hore* of green leaves is 30 to 40 kg each*, while a *kalli* of dry leaves is 20 to 30 kg each*)

Paddy straw Rs. 100 per tonne
(Each *hore* weighs 40 kg approximately)

Karada and other dry grass Rs. 100 per tonne
(Each *pindi* of grass is 2 kg approximately)

Fodder consumed during free grazing Rs. 100 per tonne**

Fencing poles and material Rs. 0.50 per pole;
Rs. 60 per tonne

Fuel wood Rs. 100 per tonne
(One headload or *hore* is 30 to 40 kg)*

Areca husk Rs. 25 per cartload

Areca hālè used for thatching Rs. 100 per thousand

* The actual weight used was as reported by the respondents.
** The quantity was estimated as explained in the section on livestock economy.

Part III

Conclusion

Chapter Eleven

Conclusion

A Synoptic View

The deterioration of our forests both in quality and quantity has been very rapid. Though the process of this deterioration could be said to have started with the British entry into the forest region, it became conspicuous at the time of the Second World War, and has continued at an accelerating pace. A study based on the visual interpretation of landsat imagery showed that even in the short period between 1972–75 and 1980–82, the forest cover in the country had gone down from 16.9 per cent of the total geographical area to 14.1 per cent.[1] The annual rate of deforestation is estimated to be a staggering figure of nearly 1.5 million hectares. We cannot conveniently blame it on droughts; nor can we afford to treat it as a technical problem concerning forest experts alone.

The problem actually lies in the political economy, which gives the rationale for this study. Though based mainly on the experience of a forest region in the Western Ghats in South India, its findings are of general interest. This is not only because the study takes note of the general context of the experience in the country as a whole, but also because in many ways the findings are illustrative of what has taken place in general, if not in every specific region.

Forests have several uses, often competing with each other. They are also scarce and becoming increasingly so in the face of pressures on them. The question of reconciling ends and scarce means cannot, however, be resolved in an air-conditioned computer room through optimisation techniques, but in the political arena of struggles between

[1] Though independently the Forest Survey of India (1981–83) estimated the forest cover to be 19.7 per cent of the geographical area, it is still far short of the needed 33 per cent. See *Wastelands News*, Vol. 3(2), November 1987–January 1988, p. 8.

the interested parties each with their own priorities or valuation of different uses or functions. The actual use of forests is determined through this struggle, and some uses which are not strongly backed are sacrificed in the process.

Among the interested parties, we have first the locals who live in the forest region, and look upon forests as a source of land for extending cultivation and supporting it through leaf manure and fodder, and also as a source of wood for fuel and other needs. A basic feature of their use of forests is that it takes place outside the market framework. The locals are not a homogeneous group, and the advantage a class derives from forests is determined by the magnitude of assets—particularly better endowed land—it controls, in spite of the non-commercialised character of forest use. It is important to note that the local use of forests is not just for survival or to meet subsistence needs alone. In the region studied, which is not a tribal region, it was largely to meet the requirements of a highly commercialised garden crop. Though landless labour also derived some benefits from forests, it was insignificant in the total forest use by the locals.

With technical changes in the larger economy, commercial and industrial interests emerged which perceived forests as a source of raw material. They forced an integration of the forest region into the larger economy which conflicted with local interests. Having arrived historically as an integral part of colonialism, they did not care for their own long-term interests of ensuring supplies in future on a sustainable basis. But, even after independence, industrial interests scarcely showed a more enlightened long-term view of forests. Though they made use of forests within a market framework, it was not based on a proper perception of the scarcity of *in situ* forest resources. Pricing was hardly based on any such perception of scarcity, and involved only a nominal payment of royalty to the owners of the land, that is, the state.

The state or its concrete form—the government—is the third interested party but its interests have been conflicting. The modern state has always been concerned with maximising the rate of economic growth which needed natural resources. To that extent, its interests coincided and even colluded with commercial interests. But even under colonialism, on the eve of the establishment of the Forest Department, it was concerned with long-term interests and assumed the responsibility to ensure a sustainable use of forests. In its role as 'conservator of forests', it had to regulate the use of forests by the other two parties, and promote regeneration and environmental care in forests treated as reserved. Thus, officially, the function of forests in safeguarding environmental balance has constituted the main interest of the state, which conflicted both with the local and commercial interests. It should also be noted that even in the colonial days the state was aware of the complementarity between forests and agriculture, and did not want to deprive the locals of all access to forests, so as to maintain the revenue potential of agriculture and to keep local unrest on account of forest regulation to the minimum. While, however, the state was pressurised both by the locals and the larger economy—particularly the latter—to meet their respective short-term needs, there was no such political pressure in the interest of conservation and sustainable use of forests even from the locals, at least not till recently. The adverse effect on the health of forests was thus inevitable.

It has often been claimed that the locals have an inherent long-term interest in forests which ensures their sustainability and conservation, and that since the state—the Forest Department included—acts under the pressure of commercial interests, it cannot ensure a sustainable use of forests. On this plea, any state regulation of local access to forests is opposed. It has been contended that there was a tradition of sustainable use of forests through community management by the locals before the British took over forests and alienated the locals. The subsequent process of deforestation is directly attributed to this alienation.

The findings of this study, however, run counter to such a claim. The locals have hardly shown any more concern for the environment than private commercial interests even in forests where they enjoyed free access. Nor was the local use of forests equitable, since the greater share of local access to forests was cornered by the local elite rather than by the local poor. In the long drawn struggles against the Forest Department, the locals rarely raised any environmental issue or gave any evidence of such awareness. If the local use of forests in the pre-commercial past was sustainable, it seems to have been due more to the limited commercial pressures from the larger economy than to the environmentally sound local practices. At the present stage of economic development, going back to an earlier—supposedly idyllic—stage of exclusive local use and denying any right to the larger economy even to protect the forests against extravagance is just not possible, just as a purely policing, bureaucratic and oppressive regulation of local use is not meaningful.

We can conceptualise four historical stages in forest use and management. During the pre-commercial-cum-pre-capitalist stage, forest use was largely local and within a non-market framework and forest resources were considered to be by and large abundant. By modern standards, the use of forests was extravagant; yet there was no major threat to the health of forests, as the pressure on them was still limited. With the integration of the forest region into the larger economy, commercial interests began to exert pressure on forest use. During the initial stage of commercialisation, which is the second stage, the demand was mainly for timber or hardwood. At the next, more advanced stage and with the entry of industrial capitalism, demand was created for softwood as a raw material for the paper and pulp industry. The increasing pressure and commercial demand meant that forest resources could no longer be considered abundant by the larger economy, and increasing scarcity began to be felt. Such scarcity could not be overcome solely through restrictions on local use to check their extravagance. It could be overcome only through a sustainable commercial and industrial use, providing for adequate regeneration as well. The indirect cost of deforestation on economic growth began to be felt elsewhere, as, for example, the higher than expected rates of siltation reducing the life of river valley projects and increasing flood-proneness of rivers. This realisation, arising out of pressure on forests, leads to an enlightened stage of forest use, where forest resources are managed from the wider perspective of long-term sustainability, and both the locals and the larger economy develop a stake in environmentally sound management.

Though these stages can theoretically be expected to be in a chronological order, their main purpose here is analytical, and their application to a forest region like the area studied to empirically identify concrete corresponding stages shows important overlaps. First, the local communities dependent on forests for local use within a non-market framework continued to exist right through the advanced stage of industrial use of forests. Using forests outside the market framework, the locals do not share the perception of scarcity by the larger economy. Yet, their non-commercialised dependence on forests continues to be vital to the local economy. The integration of the forest region into the larger economy could not eliminate such a local economy, and both non-commercialised and commercialised use have continued to co-exist. In the forest region studied, the alleged alienation of locals from the forest regions did not take place, mainly because the locals here—not being tribals—were not politically weak, and could exercise sufficient pressure though prolonged struggles against the Forest Department. They did not allow their access to forests to be prevented to such an extent as to adversely affect their economy. As a result, the locals not only secured more or less complete access to 'minor', 'village' and other 'protected' forests, but also certain privileges in 'reserved' forests that were supposed to be under complete state control.

Second, attempts at scientific management of forests to make a sustainable use of them need not appear chronologically at the final stage. In the region studied here and in the country as a whole, the state took the initiative to conserve and regenerate forests, even at the initial stage of commercialisation. In fact, it is these steps which led to greater conflicts with the locals in the region studied, more than the commercial demand on forests. However, these efforts were confined mainly to reserved forests which were under state control, and no organisation or institution was evolved to make a sustainable use of 'protected' forests where the locals had a free access. In spite of the increasing commercial demands, the reserved forests today are in a much better state of health, while the minor forests and *bettas* which were under local use are more or less completely degraded.

The relatively higher state of degradation of forests under local access cannot be attributed solely to their inadequacy in relation to demand, that is, to their being smaller in proportion than the reserved forests. It cannot also be attributed to their being inferior when they were assigned to the locals. Complaints were made from time to time during the course of local struggles against the Forest Department that only inferior or degraded forests had been assigned for use by the locals. Actually they were community forests already under people's use and located near their settlements, and much of their degradation was brought about by the locals themselves through free grazing and the practice of putting these forests deliberately on fire to promote grass cover, destroy bushes and keep away wild animals and mosquitoes. Even *betta* lands, that is, government owned forests under exclusive use of gardeners, did not escape higher degradation compared to reserved forests. Though the timber in *betta* lands was technically government property, the gardeners had the right to cut their branches for leaf manure, fodder and fuel. But this was not a sufficient incentive for them to assume the responsibility for regeneration. It was always the government that was expected to take care of regeneration and not the people even in privatised forests. The scarcity was hoped to be overcome through demanding more access to government forests or through an unauthorised use of these forests. The real alienation of people was not from forest use as such, as it was from the regeneration and management of forests. This alienation from management, though understandable in the case of reserved forests, was hardly forced on them in the case of protected forests including *bettas* and in village and other community forests. The local demand as far as community forest lands were concerned, was to hand them over for private cultivation rather than to regenerate them for common use on a sustainable basis. Politicians pretending to protect local interests put more pressure on behalf of privatisation than for evolving community management of forests under local use.

In spite of the degraded state of forests and *bettas*, their contribution to the local economy even today is quite significant. A summary view of the political economy of local dependence on forests and its relation with the control on land under private control is presented in Table 11.1. This is based on different tables in the preceding chapters. It shows that on the whole, in the surveyed villages of Uttara Kannada, the imputed value of forest produce used by them as a proportion of their total income amounted to 15.5 per cent for all households on an average, and 11.9 per cent in the case of landless labour. Similarly, taking all households together, 95 per cent of their fuel wood consumption, 75 per cent of grass and nearly 100 per cent of their leaf manure needs are met by forests including *bettas* (see Table 10.1). Their livestock economy is made viable only because of free grazing in these forests. If the imputed value of fodder from the forests is added to the costs, the net return from livestock is negative for all classes including the richest (see Table 9.2). The social cost of free grazing is more than the imputed value of fodder consumed free in community lands, since it necessitates an increase in fencing and trenching costs and tends to reduce double cropping and comes in the way of regeneration efforts everywhere particularly in community forests. Even in the case of areca gardens, one-third of their total cost is met free of charge by forests including *bettas* (see Table 8.1). The major beneficiaries of this forest use are the richer classes. The two richest classes have cornered two-thirds of even land encroached from the forests, though they constituted only 30 per cent of the households (see Table 11.1). The indifference of the locals to regenerate forests under common use could be attributed mainly to this class differentiation and to the highly skewed control on land and benefits from the forests. The

Table 11.1 Political Economy of Local Dependence on Forests: A Summary View (in the Four Villages surveyed in Uttara Kannada)

Class of Rural Households	*Percentage share of each class in total –*								*Imputed Income from Forest*	
	No. of Households	*Garden Land*	*Paddy Land*	*Grass Land*	Betta *Forest*	*Total Land*	*Encroached Land*	*Live Stock**	*Rs. Per Household*	*As Per cent of Total Income*
Landlords	15.2	61.1	33.3	58.1	65.1	58.7	35.6	37.5	11,906	13.7
Capitalist farmers	15.2	26.3	26.1	25.2	27.7	27.2	30.9	20.8	6,537	17.2
Middle peasants	4.3	4.9	4.1	3.9	6.0	5.2	8.0	4.7	3,799	18.1
Poor peasants	27.2	7.2	35.4	12.6	1.3	8.5	24.2	27.4	2,853	24.3
Agricultural labour	33.7	—	—	—	—	—	—	8.3	1,058	11.9
Service class	4.3	0.5	1.1	0.2	—	0.4	1.3	1.3	956	9.8
All	100	100	100	100	100	100	100	100	4,163	15.5

Note: * Cattle and buffaloes including calves.

influence of the highly commercialised nature of both the larger and the local economies, if not of forest use, also meant more emphasis on privatisation than on regeneration. This was not congenial for evolving local institutions for community management.

Though the two richest classes are the greatest beneficiaries in absolute terms and in terms of the share of the class in total benefits from forest use, the poor peasants are the greatest beneficiaries in terms of their own income. The poor peasants derive the largest share of their total income from forest use. In this sense, forest use is particularly significant to the poor peasants with little land. For poor peasants and landless labour, forest use is a matter of survival, while it is a matter of making high profits for the local rich.

There are no immediate prospects of any reduction in the local pressure on forests, since the region's economy is not diversified, and for the bulk of the population, agriculture still remains the major source of livelihood. While only about 10 per cent of the area of Uttara Kannada is under cultivation (over 80 per cent being forests), the bulk—60 per cent male and 70 per cent female—of the workforce has to depend on this narrow base. Though forest based industries have been set up in the region, they are mainly capital-intensive and have contributed little by way of providing employment opportunities and reducing the local pressure on forests, while their own pressure on forests for raw material continues to be significant. It should be noted, however, that in Karnataka, the demand on forests for household consumption of fuel wood far exceeds the industrial demand for raw material. However, all demand for fuel wood is not 'local'; much of it is from the larger economy and is commercialised.

Though reserved forests are in a much better state of health than other forests, their own production has hardly been heartening. On the one hand, development projects have been claiming vast areas of forests. On the other hand, the heavy pressures on forests both by the locals and industries have been degrading them. Many forest based industries launched with enthusiasm and with state encouragement, are operating below capacity due to the shortage of raw material. The industries did not take much interest in regeneration either, as they could get their raw material from the government at nominal prices which were far below the cost of regeneration. Fortunately, the price policy has been drastically revised to remedy this. But the damage has already been done. An indication of the degraded state of forests comes from the fact that in Karnataka, the State Domestic Product

(SDP) originating from forestry and logging measured at constant prices (with 1970–71 as base) declined continuously from Rs. 41 crores in 1970–71 to Rs. 31 crores in 1980–81. Even in the country as a whole, the contribution of forestry and logging at 1970–71 prices declined from Rs. 397 crores in 1970–71 to Rs. 321 crores in 1980–81 and further to Rs. 288 crores in 1985–86. In spite of the much higher increase in the prices of forestry products,[2] the contribution of this sector to the total domestic product at current prices remains very small. It actually declined from 2.1 per cent in 1970–71 to 1.9 per cent in 1980–81 in Karnataka, while in the country as a whole, it declined from 1.2 per cent to 1.0 per cent during the same period and again to 0.9 per cent in 1985–86. The controversy over production forestry as against conservation forestry seems a far cry in the face of failure on both fronts—conservation as well as production. Both, after all, are strongly correlated with each other.

This dismal picture indicates that even the state, the most responsible, powerful and farsighted of the three parties involved, failed in its task. As discussed earlier, this failure was on several counts. The state—inclusive of the Forest Department—developed a purely bureaucratic attitude to forests treating it as a purely technical problem and created a great divide between itself and the local people. Second, it failed to develop a proper data base which affected its capacity to monitor the state of forests and trends therein. Third, its own perception of the scarcity of *in situ* forest resources was hardly scientific and conservation oriented. These factors in turn accounted for the fact that the Forest Department was swept off its feet against the flood of pressure from the larger economy particularly after the Second World War if not before.

Policy Issues

Ultimately even a political economy favouring unsustainable use can

[2] The implicit price index (deflator) used in the National Accounts of India, with 1970–71 = 100 as base, stood at 223 in 1980–81 and 316 in 1985–86 for the net domestic product (total); for the forestry sector, it increased to 321 and sharply to 606 during the same years respectively. (Derived from National Accounts data, *Indian agriculture in brief*, 21st edition, 1987, pp. 5, 6).

be altered by arousing public conscience. The cause of environmental balance and sustainable resource use has suffered mainly because of the lack of a political backing. One of the most encouraging developments in recent years has been the rise of voluntary movements espousing this cause. The backing given by the government to this cause is in no small measure due to the success of these movements. This is also reflected in the Draft of the Revised National Forest Policy circulated in 1987 which has stated clearly: 'The principal aim of Forest Policy must be to ensure environmental stability and ecological balance including atmospheric equilibrium which are vital to sustenance of all life forms, human, animal and plant. The derivation of diverse economic benefit must be subordinated to this principal aim'. Popular movements will continue to be relevant in future, mainly to ensure that this principal aim will in actual practice guide forest management and use.

There can be no dispute about the fact that the concern of overall environment should be the first and foremost task of forest management, rather than productivity of forests in the narrow sense of annual increment per hectare. Yet, the situation is such that unless the productivity of forests is raised enough to meet the overall demands of the economy, the environment itself would be in danger. A wide and continuing gap between demand and supply would put tremendous pressures on forest stocks leading to their decimation. It is necessary to bear in mind that it is not a question of meeting local needs only. When the demand for fuel wood in the larger economy itself is higher, the local poor would be tempted to remove wood from forests far beyond local needs and would be prepared to undertake the necessary risks to sell it to the larger economy in spite of deterrents. We have observed earlier how the demand for fuel wood far exceeds the industrial demand for wood. The environmental protection cannot in such a situation be realised by merely opposing commercial production in forest lands.

Fortunately, the dilemma can be resolved thanks to the size of the country and the significant amount of wastelands which are neither under tree cover nor under the plough. The earlier Forest Policy (1952) had tried to meet the problem by classifying forests according to their specific functions. The environmentally sensitive forests were to be protected and preserved, while 'national' and village forests were meant to meet the needs of the larger economy and local needs respectively. Unfortunately, since forests in the first category were richest in terms of the production potential, the temptation was too strong to use them for commercial exploitation rather than conservation. The new Draft National Forest Policy (1987) reiterates almost the same strategy of classification. It says:

> *In the hills and in mountainous regions, the aim should be to maintain two-thirds of the area under such cover in order to prevent erosion and land degradation and to ensure the stability of the fragile eco-system. A massive need-based and time-bound programme of afforestation and tree planting, with particular emphasis on fuel wood and fodder development on all degraded and denuded lands in the country, whether forest or non-forest land, is a national imperative.*

Obviously, the sensitive mountainous areas will not be operated for commercial purposes, while other forest areas developed through afforestation would be expected to meet the needs of both the locals and the larger economy.

If the former areas are reserved solely for environmental protection, can they permit free access to locals? This indeed is the bone of contention between 'official' and 'popular' standpoints. If the findings of this study are any indication, locals cannot be trusted to protect the environment any more than commercial interests, though a distinction may have to be made between forests with tribals inhabiting them and other forests. Our study region comes under the latter category. The 1987 Draft Policy states: 'In order to discourage indiscriminate entry of people in the forests, forest produce and substitute materials may be distributed through depots to be established by the State Government'. In fact, several forest officers have expressed the opinion that the social cost of giving free fuel wood and fodder to the locals through depots would be much less than giving them free access to collect it themselves. Such a view has been criticised on the ground that these restrictions impinge on the rights of tribals, and strengthens bureaucratic machinery and corruption and that while the state has failed to protect forests, improvement initiatives to protect them have come from people's voluntary groups.[3]

It is important to bear in mind that the same institutions need not be suitable for forests reserved for environmental protection and other forests. While the role of the Forest Department would have to be

[3] *Cf.* Madhav Gadgil and Ramachandra Guha, 'New Forest Policy—Two steps forward, one step back?', *The Statesman*, 24 February 1988.

significant in the former involving the monitoring of the state of their health and proper regulation of local access, the role of the locals would be more important in the latter. If the state has failed in protecting the quality and quantity of reserve forests, it does not mean that the locals would be in a better position to do so if these forests are handed over to them. In fact, minor and village forests were in the hands of the locals, but these forests are almost totally decimated today and only reserved forests have remained. Though reserved forests also deteriorated, it was not because the Forest Department was not qualified and oriented to preventing it, but because it was hardly helped either by the locals or by the larger economy in this task. On the other hand, it had to continuously resist relentless pressures from both sides. Now that both the locals and the larger economy are more favourably disposed to environmental conservation, the Department should certainly be in a better position than in the past to carry out the task of conservation for which it was set up.

But to ensure that the Department does carry out this task and does not fall a prey to commercial temptations, it is necessary to independently monitor the state of health of forests with the help of eminent environmentalists. Though satellite imagery is helpful in this regard, this information should be made available for public scrutiny and analysis or assessment by environmentalists. However, changing the nature of the Department itself through inducting local politicians and making it 'popular' in this way, may hardly serve the purpose and may even prove counter-productive. But this should not prevent the Department from involving the locals at various levels and making them aware of the benefits they would enjoy from environmental protection. Interactions with the locals even in the matter of protecting and managing reserved forests would be very useful. This would mean that denying all local access to reserved forests may not be practicable, particularly in tribal areas. Grazing in reserved forests cannot be regulated merely through punitive measures, but only through the co-operation of locals. Some amount of grazing under regulated conditions where trees have attained a certain height, is actually desirable since it can minimise fire hazards. Such access, as needs to be permitted, will have to be monitored closely, preferably with the help of local committees of people.

The task of afforestation in degraded forests and wastelands would be far more challenging. It is here that people's involvement would be needed most and new institutions evolved to manage this task, since it is too formidable a task for the Forest Department alone. Fortunately, the economic environment for this is much more favourable today than in the past, thanks to the revision of the basis of pricing forest produce. As long as the price of wood remained below the cost of regeneration, there was no scope for an economic incentive to regenerate. Even the market price of minor produce like tamarind is so attractive that there is an incentive to grow trees for usufruct, apart from timber. Such trees take a long time to yield fruit. The more urgent task is to raise as much fuel wood as possible in the shortest possible time. though other needs including the need to achieve greater diversity in tree wealth certainly cannot be ignored at the same time.

This new economic environment and the rise in the market prices of fuel wood has induced many farmers to divert part of their private holdings to commercial forestry, especially eucalyptus and casurina cultivation, a development which has been bitterly criticised by a few environmentalists.[4] Apart from the possible adverse ecological impact of large scale eucalyptus cultivation (by way of a decline in groundwater and biological diversity, etc.), a significant reduction in the area under annual crop like *ragi* (consumed mainly by the poor) which is feared to have taken place in the context, is expected to reduce employment in agriculture and increase poverty. Several critics feel that such a development under 'social forestry' schemes, intended to increase a free supply of fuel and fodder for the poor, is both ironic and poignant. Thanks to this criticism, though in the initial days, the Forest Department had encouraged eucalyptus cultivation in private holdings, it has now stopped even raising eucalyptus seedlings in its nurseries, at least in Karnataka. However, farmers buy seedlings from private nurseries and receive a part of their payment in advance from merchants or industry. Farmers also raise casurina to supply to private timber and fuel wood depots. Thus farmers or private agricultural holdings are becoming a significant source of raw material for industry as well as of fuel wood for the larger economy.

[4] Vandana Shiva, H.C. Sharatchandra and J. Bandyopadhyay, 'Social, economic and ecological impact of social forestry in Kolar', Indian Institute of Management, Bangalore, 1981 (Mimeo); Vandana Shiva, S.T. Somasekhara Reddy and J. Bandyopadhyay, 'The ecology of eucalyptus and farm forestry policy in rainfed areas, in Indian Statistical Institute, *Workshop on eucalyptus plantation—Papers and proceedings*, Bangalore, 1984, pp. 201–32; B.V. Krishnamurthy, 'Ecological destruction through government policies', *ibid.*, pp. 10–18.

These developments have, however, taken place in the semi-arid tracts in South Karnataka and not in the Western Ghats, since it is only in the former region that farm forestry is more attractive than substitute crops which have low and uncertain yields. In such a context, this is not necessarily a negative development. In a way this development is a welcome—even if late—corrective to the unplanned expansion of private holdings into areas unsuitable for cultivation. Such areas created little employment as it is, because even if *ragi* was displaced in the process, its cultivation was barely a source of much employment. Moreover, though the area under *ragi* has declined in Karnataka over the years, its output has tended to increase (except during severe droughts) due to the success of high yielding varieties in rainfed areas. A more intensive cultivation of areas suited for it, and the diversion of agricultural land for agro-forestry in areas unsuitable for annual crops, would amount to a more rational land use. Some restrictions will have to be imposed on the diversion of good agricultural land for the purpose, particularly if wood prices continue to increase significantly. A race between food and wood prices can ruin the landless weaker sections.

The adverse ecological impact of eucalyptus cultivation need not be feared, provided there is no 'eucalyptisation of India' or of whole regions against which J. Bandyopadhyay has rightly cautioned. A source of concern from the farmers' viewpoint, however, is the possibility of an artificially induced crash in prices to suit industrial or trade interests, and exploitation by middlemen. A price guarantee by the Forest Department is, on the other hand, liable to be interpreted as undue encouragement to grow softwood needed by trade and industry, as against the non-commercial needs of people. Growers of softwood would have to be organised on a co-operative basis for selling their produce to trade and industry to prevent exploitation.

It is not necessary for farmers to devote an area exclusively for forestry. It is possible to resort to what is known as alley cropping, where field crops are raised between rows of trees and shrubs which do not have a large crown and as such are not shady, but nevertheless produce fodder and fuel. There are many varieties which by fixing nitrogen in the soil, actually increase crop yields and complement agriculture. Their roots absorb moisture from greater depths than field crops, and as such do not compete with the latter. They can arrest soil erosion and even improve the moisture retention of farm land. These systems combining farm forestry with annual field crops enable farmers to have quicker returns than from farm forestry alone, and are ecologically preferable. These systems, however, may not be practicable on small and fragmented holdings.

Though the use of parts of private holdings for quick growing trees is welcome within limits, handing over degraded government forest lands to private parties or farmers for the purpose is another matter and cannot be socially justified unless such lands are temporarily leased—not sold—for the limited purpose of enjoying usufructs. The government does not have the machinery to ensure that the forest holdings would in fact be used for the purpose expected and to prevent their transfer to the more powerful classes, even if initially such holdings are given only to the weaker sections of rural society. Moreover, it would be naive to expect that the produce of such forest holdings, even if raised with trees, would be used to meet the subsistence needs of the weaker sections. It is quite likely that these holdings may not be used productively for the purpose meant, but only to consolidate the position of the elite. Even as it is, large private holdings leave considerable land uncultivated and without any tree cover. If government forest lands are parcelled out and distributed on a large scale, in course of time all forest lands may vanish under the pressure of population and livestock, and only private agricultural holdings will remain. The entire burden of meeting the non-commercial local needs would again fall on the reserved forests. The moral of Govind Nihalani's serial, Tamas, 'Those who forget history will be condemned to repeat it', is relevant here too.

The experience of Uttara Kannada in the case of *betta* lands shows that even when exclusive rights on usufruct are given, it is not an adequate incentive to grow trees. This was in spite of the fact that conditions were laid down initially that the *bettas* would be maintained well, with the necessary tree cover. The Forest Department had neither the means nor the interest to compel *betta* holders to respect these conditions, and to takeover the *bettas* when these conditions were not fulfilled. One wonders whether this is unique to Uttara Kannada, and whether it is not likely to be repeated in the tree patta schemes under which land can be leased to give exclusive usufructuary rights (see Chapter 6). The difference lies in the fact that *bettas* were in effect under free private possession being tied to the ownership of arecanut gardens, though formally the government owned them along with nominal rights on timber when the trees were felled. Under tree pattas, land is leased for the limited purpose of *growing* trees, with no rights on land for the patta holders. Similarly the patta holder has no right on timber when the tree is felled unless the land is taken over from the patta holder for a development project. There have been other schemes offering further incentive, a share of up to 50 per cent of the harvested yield for the patta holder. In the case of *bettas*, however, the holder could still have it after paying a nominal price to the government if the government did not want it and, in actual practice, it did not claim it and was satisfied with the price. Thus, *bettas* have offered more incentive for growing trees than the present tree patta scheme, and yet their degradation could not be prevented. The tree patta scheme being much less attractive, has not evoked an encouraging response. What then could be the other institutions for refforestation of the denuded government forests?

If it is not desirable to hand over government forest land to private individuals, it is even more so in the Indian context to hand them over to industrial units to raise captive plantations. Such a step would enormously increase the social, economic and political power of these units and tilt the delicate balance of political economy very much in their favour. Once such a provision is made, they will ask for and even get the richest forests that need to be preserved as has happened already; they could also tempt farmers to part with agriculturally rich lands. These uints may continue to depend on the government and private farmers to meet their needs of raw materials, and use such land for speculative purposes to build up property and money power more than for raising plantations. Even if some plantations are raised, they may use them to bargain with farmers to bring down prices. Above all, such a solution would help little in meeting the fuel wood needs even of the larger economy, let alone the non-commercial needs of the local poor. Though industrial needs have to be met, they have to be met in ways other than through the enormous captive plantations being owned by the industry itself.

We may think of two separate types of institutions, one to take care of the degraded reserved forests under the government itself, and the other to take care of minor and such other forests including *bettas* which are left open to the exercise of local privileges and use. The first category of forests may be given over to the Forest Plantation Corporation under the public sector to develop forestry on businesslike and environmentally sound principles. They can meet the fuel wood requirements of the larger economy including softwood for industry, while giving priority to the former. Such a corporation can have the advantage of meeting its investment needs through loans from public sector banks, which the Forest Department does not enjoy.[5] Even if operated professionally, they can still meet a part of the non-commercial needs of the locals for fuel in the vicinity of the plantations. The ecologically sensitive regions, even if already degraded, would have to be under the Department itself for promoting regeneration and conservation, and not under commercial forestry.

Minor and such other forests which could be called people's forests could be brought under co-operative community management, providing for equal rights to the produce of the forests irrespective of the size of holdings and including the landless for the purpose on the same lines as followed in the case of Pani Panchayat for sharing water. Unless equal rights are given to all and monopolisation by the rich is prevented, regeneration would be difficult, since securing the co-operation of villagers would not be possible. These forests should be a source of leaf manure, fodder, firewood and fruits for the entire village. The Forest Department could, as the owner of the land, retain its rights over the land to safeguard against misuse and misappropriation and also help actively in planting trees and, where necessary, in enclosing such land by trenching and fencing.

Till institutions of community management are evolved, the initial help and investment by the Forest Department would be crucial for success. In fact, initiative may have to be taken by the Department itself or by voluntary non-government organisations for securing community co-operation and evolving popular institutions. Minor and such other forests could not be regenerated earlier because such external help was not forthcoming, and the Department had not shown such initiative and interest. A start has already been made in Uttara Kannada where the Department has enclosed parts of minor forests on a rotational basis and has raised live fencing. At the initial stages, it encountered some resistance, but the locals eventually supported the scheme as they were promised a share in the produce of such forests in return for their co-operation. The expenses on trenching and fencing can be recovered within a period of three to four years in the form of imputed value of firewood raised through live fencing alone. Tens of hectares of degraded grazing forests have been regenerated with the active co-operation of Gavlis, a nomadic grazing community. In this task of eco-development, people's own organisations, an

[5] See Nadkarni and G.V.K. Rao, *op. cit.* (see fn. 15, Ch. 6).

environmentalists' professional group under the guidance of Professor Madhav Gadgil, and the Forest Department are working together. It is an interesting model.

Fortunately there is no dearth of similar experiments elsewhere in the country including the semi-arid tracts of Karnataka. An interesting model is provided by a voluntary organisation called the Taralabalu Rural Development Foundation promoted by a religious institution—a Math—in Sirigere of Chitradurga district. Their area of operation is a droughtprone tract. Beginning with the schools and colleges, started by the Math, to promote environmental awareness and tree growing through nurseries raised by students, the organisation gradually took the initiative to develop selected gomals—village grazing lands. About two-thirds of the gomal is left free for grazing, while the remaining one-third is enclosed for grazing on a rotational basis for a period of about four years, and trees are planted for raising fodder, fuel and fruit. The expenses are borne by the organisation with the financial support of the Society for the Promotion of Wastelands Development, while committees of villagers are set up to ensure that the enclosed gomals are sustainably and equitably used by them. Within months of enclosure, the difference between an enclosed gomal and an open gomal became obvious. The growth of grass was significant enough to convince the villagers of the benefits involved. Almost all the seedlings which were planted survived, and showed signs of rapid growth.[6]

One of the most important tasks facing community management anywhere would be to ensure that there is no uncontrolled grazing and no uncontrolled harvesting of produce. Regulation of grazing is particularly important in India where the ratio of human to livestock population is 2:1, compared with 10:1 in China. Free range grazing is reported to be forbidden in China, though the pressure of livestock is much less in China than here.[7]

An effective unit for community management of grazing lands and village forests seems to be the village itself, with a population of about 1,000 to 1,500, and approximately 300 acres of community land to manage. Larger units could raise problems of effective involvement of people. However, some villages may not have so much land, and

[6] These observations are based on the author's own visits to some of these gomals. Also see Manu N. Kulkarni, 'Taralabalu seedlings—An experiment in social forestry', *Wastelands News*, Vol. 3(2), November 87–January 88, p. 13.

[7] *Cf.* Government of India, *Afforestation and peoples' involvement—A study of China's experience*, National Wastelands Development Board, Ministry of Environment and Forests, May 1987, p. 6.

others may have even more. The ratio of population to village common land varies widely. An understanding could be reached between neighbouring villages to trade surpluses in fuel wood and fodder at agreed prices after meeting their own needs, the proceeds from this sale could be utilised for village development. Lands encroached upon by middle and large farmers, both grasslands and forest lands under their exclusive private control should all be included under community lands so that each village can augment its common land resources.

The question of whether or not village management of common lands should be brought under the supervision of local government institutions at the grass-roots level like Mandal Panchayats in Karnataka, can be resolved only in the light of experience. Preferably, it should be organised separately on a co-operative basis, with all households in the village as members with equal rights. Even if they are under Panchayats, the former should be separated from the day-to-day operations of the latter so that a new bureaucracy does not stifle local initiative, and unhealthy petty politics on caste and party lines involved in power politics does not affect the management of community lands. In any case, as a check against domination by an elite class or caste, a monitoring of the functioning of village co-operatives or committees and of the use of community lands has to be periodically done independently by voluntary organisations with a larger unit of operation together with the co-operation of the Forest Department. It is imperative that guidelines are formulated for the functioning of village committees to ensure that benefits are shared equitably with the weaker sections.

These policy issues may have to be studied further, and details worked out for their implementation. What is obvious, however, is that forests can no longer be treated by private interests as an unlimited free resource for private profit. Moreover, while the Forest Department will continue to play a crucial role, it cannot take on singlehandedly the task of regenerating all the degraded forests. A desirable institutional alternative has to be found—neither giving away forests to private parties nor policing private use. The alienation of locals from the management and regeneration has to end. Fortunately, there is today immense enthusiasm about popular involvement, and there is no dearth of experiments and even of some success. The seeds have been sown, the environment for them is good as never before. and they will hopefully grow into big trees, even if they may take time to yield tangible fruit.

Index